Heading Home

BISHOP KAY WARD

Interprovincial Board of Communication
Moravian Church in North America

$\mathcal{D}$EDICATION

$\mathcal{F}$or Helen and for Ralph,

      your faithfulness has delighted me

      all of these years.

(See *Two Small Envelopes* on page 103.)

FOREWORD

To my readers —

I have been a commuter and a traveler for the past 15 years and the best part of every trip was "heading home" when my travels were at an end. Thus a title was born. Heading home has also become a metaphor for the journey that my husband and I have made by returning to our roots in retirement. After 30 years of serving congregations from coast to coast, we have returned to the community where we began our ministry in the early 70's. For the past year, we have been rediscovering people and places, made new again in retirement.

Over the years since the publishing of my last book, *Of Seasons and Sparrows*, I have loved corresponding with you, my readers. You have corrected my grammar (always appreciated), questioned my choice of biblical texts and my recollection of certain events, and you have told me your stories. Many of you have shared how you have used the stories. Some of you read the chapters with a loved one. Some of you use the stories as devotionals for committee meetings or other church gatherings. It is my prayer that you will find comfort, inspiration, and perhaps a chuckle or two in the stories in this new collection.

For those of you who recognize yourself in one of my stories or if you have had an experience exactly as I describe in a story, please forgive me. I have given myself a lot of latitude, to change names, places, make composite events and add or subtract enough details to make what I thought was a good story.

My last book went to press as we awaited the birth of our first granddaughter. We now have three splendid granddaughters, Nadia, Cecilia, and Madeline and I am keenly aware that I've only written about the oldest. There are many other omissions here, as well, but the great loves of my life should be apparent — my husband, Aden, our children and their children, our extended family, the large circle of friends, all often wend their way down the road to Wards Woods. You will also read about the things that sustain me — knitting, writing, reading, traveling, staying home, and telling stories.

Many of you, who have been to Wards Woods, will be puzzled by the picture on the front cover of this book. Some have asked whether we got our road paved for the picture. Be assured that a picture of our own road can be found on the back cover, thanks to the photographic skills of John H. Keel Photography in Wisconsin Rapids, Wisconsin.

I continue to write for the *Express Times* in Easton, Pennsylvania, where the stories in this book were originally published.

My sincere thanks to all who have been part of *Heading Home*:

> those who shared travels and stories with me
>
> those who read and proofed stories
>
> Deanna Hollenbach, Director of Communication for the Moravian Church in North America, who has served as editor
>
> Sandy Fay of Laughing Horse Graphics, Doylestown, Pennsylvania, who has served as designer

Kay Ward
October 2005

*T*ABLE *O*F *C*ONTENTS

P LACES

T IME & S PACE

$\mathcal{C}$ OMING $\mathcal{H}$ OME

GETTING THERE

DAILY WALK

*If the whole body were an eye, where would the
hearing be? If the whole body were hearing, where
would the sense of smell be? But as it is, God
arranged the members in the body, each one of
them, as he chose. 1 Corinthians 12:17-18*

I have become accustomed to taking a walk around my neighborhood early most mornings. I have a mile course and, being a creature
of habit, I usually go exactly the same route each morning.

The blocks fly by as I notice the familiar landscape. Lights are on in
most of the houses in what I assume is the kitchen area. In one
home, a black cat sleeps in a front window, pressed between drapery
and glass.

Strolling by shop windows, I choose the perfect flooring or pick out a
new stove. Window-shopping is a good distraction. Each block
becomes as familiar to me as my own front porch and sidewalk.

When winter snows arrived, it became impossible to traverse the
alleys and sidewalks. Snow banks were formed into creative winter
garages at the curb and intersections provided the special challenge
of snow banks and icy ruts.

Some time passed before sidewalks had been scraped or chopped
free of ice and snow, or warm weather eased the problem.
Eventually, I started out on my morning routine again, mindful that
the sidewalks could still be hazardous. They could still surprise with
lethal sheets of ice where you least expected it.

This caused me to walk with a very different posture. My usual custom has been to walk with my head up, enjoying all of the images I passed. Now I found myself with eyes focused on the ground ahead of me, constantly alert to any ice.

As so often happens, when my usual sense of taking in my environment was busy doing other things, my other senses went to work. One morning I heard my neighborhood for the first time. As I passed gates and yards, dogs greeted me — some in high-pitched, short yelps, and others in low, serious, foreboding alarms. I picture these dogs in my imagination. I have never seen them, but for the first time I was very aware of their existence.

I heard car doors slamming, signaling people warming up their engines to go to work. In the next block, someone was scraping frost off car windows. My ears were working overtime when I suddenly knew exactly where I was — the sweet comforting smell of bread baking directed me to the bakery near my house.

I let my nose work for a while and found it very reliable. Here was the garage for car repair. Here was the diner with the hint of fried onions. There was a house where someone was frying bacon. In the next block, someone was already doing laundry and I could smell the sweet, moist, hot smell of a dryer vent.

All of my senses are precious, but I take them for granted. It was such a blessing to experience my neighborhood by sound and smell as well as by sight.

I can't wait for spring. I know that I'll enjoy the smells of spring flowers and maybe if I really practice, I'll hear them growing as well.

God of our Senses, how did you know that we could be renewed by the perfume of growing things? We are grateful. Amen.

*T*HREE *L*ENTEN *G*IFTS

For I am convinced that neither death, nor life,
nor angels, nor rulers, nor things present, nor
things to come, nor powers, nor height, nor depth,
nor anything else in all creation, will be able to
separate us from the love of God in Christ Jesus
our Lord. Romans 8:38-39

*W*ho has not looked into the eyes of a small child and struggled with the question, "Why do we call it Good Friday?" It is not an easy question to answer for a child or a grown-up. We usually answer with some very heavy theological explanation about Good Friday being part of God's plan that Jesus should die. Or we explain it by pointing to the good that comes to us at Easter from this Friday death.

Moravians observe Holy Week with daily readings from the gospels in order to participate in the last days of Jesus' life. In that keeping, I am always struck with the rhythm of the week, from the excitement and raucous celebration of Palm Sunday through each day until the quiet sadness of Maundy Thursday and Good Friday, and finally the silence of Saturday, the Great Sabbath.

It is this movement that brings us to the glory of the Easter Sunday. We gather to declare with all Christians, "He is risen, He is risen, indeed." You have to travel through Friday to get to Sunday. I know that as a Christian, as a Moravian, as a human being. That's the way it works. It is in this spirit that I want to suggest that there are three good things about Good Friday.

Good Friday reminds us of the gift of uncertainty. We say to ourselves, well, if such a terrible thing could happen to God's son, surely our lives are precarious too.

It isn't a gift that we always welcome because we want guarantees. We want control. We get angry when circumstances sneak up on us. But when I sit quietly on a dark Friday afternoon and hear again the precious words from the cross, I try to be grateful for the life that God has given us. We are not toys for God, but people who live in relationship with God. We make choices and such freedom gives us a complex life full of surprises, adventures, and yes, uncertainty.

Good Friday reminds us of the gift of imperfection. There in the garden, I see the friends gathered around Jesus, just hours away from their denial. Surely if these so-called friends could fail so miserably, I can expect that my family and friends will disappoint me too. It is human. It is inevitable. But Good Friday soothes my judgment with the gift of imperfection. When I look at those I love, I see the face of imperfection. It comforts me. It is the same face I see when I look in the mirror. On a dark Friday afternoon, as I hear the familiar words of betrayal and death, I try to be grateful for the frailty that makes us all human beings, for second chances, and for imperfection.

Good Friday reminds us of the gift of inseparability. In lives slippery with uncertainty and detoured with imperfection, I am stunned with the news that God is with us, ALWAYS. It is not God's absence that we see there at the cross, it is God's presence, full of grace and mercy.

So on the darkest day, on that awful afternoon, I can stand it. I can stand to be in that place at the foot of the cross. Once a year, I need to be there, probably more than once a year actually, and while I stand there at the cross, I thank God for the gift of Jesus Christ, for the gift of uncertainty, the gift of imperfection, and for the gift of grace and inseparability.

God of Good, you make our lives of
uncertainties and imperfection holy things.
Help us to see the good in Good Friday and
may every Friday remind us of your gift.
Amen.

WAITING IN LINES

I wait for the LORD, my soul waits,
and in his word I hope. Psalm 130:5

"*W*aiting in Line" is an appropriate theme for Advent time. Waiting in line has become an expected part of travel since September 11, 2001. Arriving at Newark Airport on the Friday before the Thanksgiving weekend was a guarantee that I would be waiting in line. As I waited at the ticket counter to get my boarding pass, I wondered how all the people in all the lines would ever be able to get through security in time for departures. The lines moved slowly, but I was impressed with the patience exhibited by my companions. No one voiced it but there was a sense that we were all participating in something slightly ominous. There was an overtone of tension and danger as we waited our turn to begin our travel.

We waited for an hour and in all that time I didn't hear anyone complain. There was a purpose to the waiting — we all wanted to be safe. I wouldn't have believed that I could stand for so long a time with so many Americans with no whining. Maybe September 11 has brought about a new kinder, gentler America. I was proud to be part of it.

Just a week later, I stood in another line, this time for 3 hours. This was a very different kind of line. My husband and I were waiting for a box office to open in order to buy tickets for Garrison Keillor's "Prairie Home Companion." This line was a totally different experience. These weren't travelers — these were neighbors — this was family. Though we didn't know each other, we all shared a common experience. We were all radio listeners signing on for an evening of delight. This line had none of the tension of the airport line. Most people came prepared. They brought their morning coffee, the newspaper, their knitting, and their cell phones. They formed a very proper line with no crowding. Some brought chairs and others dragged padded benches from the lobby. There were two kinds of people in the long line. There were those who had come for companionship so they clumped in small groups. Our clump had a man from Alaska who was visiting friends who had asked him to stand in line and get tickets for them. There was a violin teacher, a mother who home-schooled, and a woman who worked for public radio. The three hours passed quickly as we chatted.

The other group was made up of people who didn't need conversation, at least that early in the morning or with total strangers. They set themselves very carefully in place, establishing a safe space around themselves, whether they stood or were seated on the floor or on a chair. They read their books or newspapers with total concentration and seemed oblivious to the crowd around them.

I've spent a lot of time standing in line lately and at least in the places I have been, the American character seems to be healthy and strong. Waiting in line also has a lot to do with what we are waiting for. Are we waiting for an airplane ride that might be making us a little nervous or are we waiting for tickets for an evening of radio theater?

As we wait in line in these next hectic weeks of Advent, may we think about the One that we wait for — that holy One born in a manger — that holy One who can bring peace to a world that knows so little peace. Blessings on our Advent waiting!

Patient God, we are not always patient when we have to wait for small things as well as big things. Make of our waiting a blessing. Amen.

$\mathcal{T}$WO $\mathcal{M}$EN

But it is not so among you; but whoever wishes to become great among you must be your servant, and whoever wishes to be first among you must be slave of all. Mark 10:43-44

*T*his is a story of two men — one man that I never met and one man that I knew. It is a story of ego and humility — a tale of being first and being last. I heard about the first man from a flight attendant while we were both waiting for our flight to arrive at a big airport. This is her story — an urban legend if ever I heard one.

It was one of those terrible flying days when flights had been delayed or cancelled because of weather and long lines snaked back from each gate counter as people tried to get rescheduled. At one of the gates, at the end of a particularly long line, there was a commotion. A well-dressed businessman, in a three-piece suit, was complaining loudly about his missed flight. The people around him were beginning to get uncomfortable with his behavior as he got more and more agitated. His voice grew louder as he described the meeting that he was missing and how someone was going to pay for this delay. Suddenly he could stand it no longer and barged up to the counter. He shoved a woman aside as he took his place in front of the gate attendant and slammed his fist on the counter. Putting his face just inches from the face of the gate attendant, he said, "Do you know who I am?" Without saying a word, the harried young woman reached for the phone and her voice came over the loudspeaker, "May I have your attention please? There is a man here at Gate 20 who doesn't seem to know who he is. Would someone please come and identify him?" The crowd burst into applause and the man slunk to the end of the line.

I met the second man when we moved to a new parish a couple of years ago. Fred was the official greeter of the congregation no matter who else was assigned to be the greeter for the morning. Fred had a friendly handshake for all who entered, but that was just a small part of his responsibilities for the Sunday worship service. Fred opened up the church, he turned on the lights, he straightened up the sanctuary, and just before the service began, he placed a fresh glass of water on the pulpit. And that was only on Sunday. Fred was at the church every day doing those things that no one else noticed needed to be done. Fred had retired several times from the furniture store where he spent his entire career as a salesman. Fred could remember every customer even if they came into the store years after a purchase and he would remember what they had bought. He loved people and cared enough to remember the details of their life that made them unique. This past Christmas Eve, he was at his usual place after the Christmas Eve service with a little bag of candy and fruit for each and every child.

Fred died four days after Christmas and the church was filled to overflowing for his memorial service. The family greeted friends, business associates, and members of the congregation and people smiled as they told their favorite story about Fred. It was his grandson that summed up Fred's life for all of us. He told of his grandfather keeping in touch with all his grandchildren and of how he had helped him buy a car. He ended by saying, "in his whole life, Grandpa was always putting someone else in front of himself."

Two men — two stories.

This is the Word of the Lord.

> *God, you are alpha and omega — the first and*
> *the last. Help us to be clear about our place in*
> *your kingdom, whether we are first or last,*
> *and may we know your will for us. Amen.*

THE CRUISE

*But just as we have been approved by God to be
entrusted with the message of the gospel, even so
we speak, not to please mortals, but to please God
who tests our hearts. 1 Thessalonians 2:4-5*

Last February, I went on a cruise. I am not exactly a cruise kind of
person, but my friend invited me to celebrate our 60th birthdays
together and I said yes.

One morning, as we were getting ready to go to breakfast, the
captain came over the loudspeaker. He said, "We have received a
mayday from a ship in distress and must go there to see how we
may be of help."

By the time we made it to the dining room, the ship had arrived at
the scene. In addition to our cruise ship there was a large container
ship and an oil rigger. Again the captain's voice came over the loudspeaker. "The ship is a marine biology research ship and is taking
on water. All personnel have been rescued and are safe. We will stay
in attendance."

For the next two hours, most of the passengers on our ship stood on
deck or at windows to watch the ship sink. Folks were very quiet.
When the last bit of the ship had slipped below the water, all that
remained was an oil slick and a rubber raft. The captain blew three
long, mournful blasts of the ship's horn. I looked around me and
many were in tears. "Did you see the name of the ship? — it was
called the Aloha."

What I sensed from my fellow passengers is that there was a huge
capacity for ritual, symbol, and sign among these probably mostly

un-churched folks. Their hunger drew them to the side of the ship to experience this event. And I, firmly planted in the church, wanted to say — you want ritual, symbol, and sign? We have it every Sunday. It is there for the taking. We know about attending — we sit with the dying. We know about ritual. We know about sacrament — we take the bread and wine.

Sometimes I even say these things to the world from inside the door of the church. I invite them in, but they mostly shake their heads and look for meaning for their lives elsewhere.

On one of the cruise excursions, we spent a delightful day with a couple from Long Island. We talked of children and of vacations — safe topics like you do with strangers. At the end of the day, the husband came up to my friend and me and asked if he could ask a question. We said, "Sure." He said, "Are you nuns?" We said, "no — but we are churchwomen, ordained clergywomen. Why do you ask?"

"Well," he said, "when we were talking about our next cruise we mentioned leaving in a week for Mardi Gras and you both snapped to and said, 'No, Lent doesn't start until two weeks from now.' We figured that the only people who would know when Lent started were nuns."

And I, firmly planted in the church, wanted to say — how is it that you don't know about our calendar when we take it so seriously? You not only don't care what we do but you live by a completely different calendar.

I want to care enough about those people on the ship to offer them the saving power of Jesus Christ who gives meaning to life. I want to go about the business of being in the church so gracefully that my neighbors, noticing that I have a different rhythm of my life, will fall in step with that rhythm, naturally and freely. I want to live my life so joyfully that the world will ask where that joy comes from and I will be compelled to tell them about the Savior. I want to do all these things. It's a work in progress.

> *God of Good News, strengthen our good*
> *intentions to share your good news with*
> *others. When we get too busy or too shy, make*
> *our sharing tender and gracious. Amen.*

_T_RAVELING _B_Y _T_RAIN

I am the gate. Whoever enters by me will be saved,
and will come in and go out and find pasture.
The thief comes only to steal and kill
and destroy. I came that they may have life,
and have it abundantly. John 10:9-10

_I_ am writing this on an airplane — a very small airplane. I am wedged into a seat next to a large gentleman who is trying to settle in. He is very polite and is making every effort to not invade my space but on an airplane like this, everyone's space is invaded. He turns on his light. He adjusts the airflow. I get light and airflow whether I need it or not.

Air travel these days is governed by security and the bottom line. And I'm sure the bottom line dictates that we cram ourselves into the smallest planes to keep airfares as low as possible. I'm not complaining — I appreciate the low fares and the service. I am a satisfied frequent flyer. However, I did get a little spoiled a few weeks ago when my husband and I took a trip from Chicago to Washington D.C. on a train. I couldn't help but make a few comparisons.

On an airplane, everyone has a computer case and a cell phone and they are in a hurry.

On a train, everyone has their bag of snacks and a good book and they will get there eventually, when the train rolls into the station.

On a plane, business people in three-piece-suits try to stay looking good for their meeting the minute the plane lands.

On trains, families in blue jeans and sweat suits and fuzzy slippers are looking forward to a visit with grandma or in our case, a visit with a granddaughter.

On a plane, you receive a four-inch package containing three almonds and three pretzels and a drink with lots of ice and very little soda.

On a train, you order a three-course meal in the dining car seated at a table with a linen tablecloth.

On a plane, since everyone is so crowded together, people do their best to maintain some kind of privacy.

On a train, getting to know one another is encouraged. In the dining car, you're seated with people you don't know and most folks engage in conversation. You greet these new friends later when you see them in the observation car or even later in the train station.

The obvious difference of course, is that I was on a long distance train for a full 24 hours. When people board the train, they find a seat, cozy themselves into a little nest, and wrap themselves in their afghan from the couch at home. People don't do that on an airplane.

Both of these modes of travel are essential and I do love the speed of air travel — it gets me where I need to be. But I hope that we don't lose train travel in this country. There is something therapeutic about sitting on a train and watching the world go by, rather slowly. The world seen from a train is not always pretty — there is stunning honesty sometimes. Small towns show beautiful front porches to cars as they pass but on a train, you see the alleys and backyards. Trains expose the under-bellies of our towns and villages. Big cities raise their tall buildings that can be seen from the air, but trains see the rusty hulks of empty warehouses. And I have to say, I enjoyed it and I can't wait to do it again.

Train travel reminds me that it isn't only the arrival that is important but the getting there. It's all about that balance between getting the job done and taking time to live life fully.

All aboard!

God of all our Journeys, grant us travel mercies and the wisdom and grace to enjoy the ride as much as the destination. Amen.

*L*OOKING *U*P *T*O *S*OMEONE

*Then the righteous will answer him, 'Lord, when
was it that we saw you hungry and gave you food,
or thirsty and gave you something to drink? And
when was it that we saw you a stranger and
welcomed you, or naked and gave you clothing?
And when was it that we saw you sick or in prison
and visited you?' And the king will answer them,
'Truly I tell you, just as you did it to one of the
least of these who are members of my family, you
did it to me. Matthew 25:37-40*

*G*reg, our 15 year-old friend, asked me to be a coach when he and his two sisters, Katie and Beth, volunteered to lead the church service a couple of weeks ago. He chose Matthew 25:40 for his text.

As his coach and considering myself a seasoned sermon writer, I came up with several directions that I thought he could go with the text. Greg was having none of it. He said that he had thought about it and he thought that the text was about how we treated people who were different from us. He thought that was what God wanted him to say about it. After he explained the text to me, I agreed with him.

And preach the text, he did. He preached that being 15 years old, 6'5", weighing 250 pounds, and being in the 9th grade, he knew a whole lot about being different. He preached about an old football player that he had heard speak. He preached about a sign that he had seen a homeless person holding — the sign said, "We all need a little help sometimes." He ended his sermon by referring to a man in our congregation.

John is middle-aged, a brilliant musician, chair of the board of elders of the congregation, and he is blind. John sits in the same pew every Sunday, halfway back on the left side of the sanctuary, next to his wife, Jill. Greg spoke to John as he concluded the sermon.

"John, you are probably the only person in this whole congregation that doesn't know that I am really tall. I am taller than almost every person in my Junior High, including the teachers. I am taller than almost every person in this congregation. Almost every place I go, people have to look up to me to talk to me. But John, you are the person that I have always looked up to. That's what we kids need — we need someone to look up to. Thank you for being that kind of man."

I spend a lot of time speaking to people about their vocation, about their call to ministry. And often, adults will ask me what they can do to encourage young people to consider a call to the ordained ministry. I think this is what I need to say from now on. Using Greg's words, I think I need to say — be the kind of people that kids can look up to. Kids need someone to look up to. They need grown-ups who live lives of faith out loud — in ways that young people can see and model. That way their faith can grow strong and they can mature into strong young adults who may be able to say "yes" when God calls.

I can't wait to see what these splendid kids grow up to be.

> *God, we are mentors whether we know it or not. Help us to remember that there are others who are watching us as we try to be your disciples. Amen.*

Y OU N EVER K NOW

The wolf shall live with the lamb,
the leopard shall lie down with the kid,
the calf and the lion and the fatling together,
and a little child shall lead them. Isaiah 11:6

T he small commuter jet was filling up as I took my place near a window and made room for my seatmate to arrive, who turned out to be a handsome, tall man in his mid 40's, with a short, trendy haircut and tanned face. As he got seated, he cheerfully greeted a man who was taking his seat across the aisle from him. It was obvious that they were not traveling together but knew each other from somewhere. I wondered whether they were both from the same hometown, the one that we were heading to? I soon found out in the following conversation.

Seat 8C — how do you like working for your new company?

Seat 8B — alright, I guess. I am doing a lot more traveling than when I worked with you guys, but it's OK. It's a living. I am glad to have a job. You just never know. Been out on the coast since the first week in January, almost 2 months. It will be good to get home. How are things with you? Same old, same old?

8C — Things aren't great. The place is a mess. The company got bought out, ya' know. Kid running things now can't be 30 years old. He loves being the big boss with us old timers.

8B — I know what you mean.

8C — I just try to get by, keeping my head down and waiting for my paycheck. I'm OK as long as they keep sending me that paycheck. Say, how are your kids?

27

8B — They drive me crazy. They hang out with friends that look like hoodlums. You just never know these days.

8C — Yea, did you hear about Lenny?

8B — You mean, that guy that used to travel with you all the time?

8C — Yea, that's the guy — well, he died.

8B — What? He was a lot younger than we are.

8C — He was 42 years old. Was just sitting in his apartment, having a pizza and a beer, watching TV and that was it. The man from upstairs came down to see him but when he didn't answer the door, he just thought he was asleep. Nobody found him till the next day. You just never know.

With this, both men turned to the newspapers they were holding and started to read intently. The dialogue that I heard is perfect airplane talk. It is the kind of conversation that takes place when words are spoken but little is being heard. Or if heard, at least not responded to. I wanted to jump into the conversation and get more information from these two good men who were just trying to make a living and were missing their families. I wanted to ask more questions about the kids and I wanted to know how it made them feel to know that their contemporary died in his chair, watching TV. But of course, this was airplane talk, so the questions were not asked.

I often imagine that the Kingdom of God would be different. The Kingdom of God would be a place where the lamb would lie down with the lion. The Kingdom of God would be a place where stranger and friend could be honest and vulnerable with each other without being afraid. The Kingdom of God — I pray for it every day.

Thy kingdom come, thy will be done on earth as it is in heaven. You just never know!

God, you call us to live deeply with you and with others. Never let us be satisfied with living on the surface of life. Amen.

PEOPLE

$\mathcal{B}$IRTH $\mathcal{O}$F $\mathcal{A}$ $\mathcal{G}$RANDDAUGHTER

We will not hide them from their children;
we will tell to the coming generation
the glorious deeds of the LORD, and his might,
and the wonders that he has done. Psalm 78:4

I am the most dangerous of all human beings. Total strangers cross the street when they see me coming. Small children wilt under my gaze. My mere presence can scare the strongest grownups. I am a new grandmother!

I am a crazed woman. Not a conversation goes by without my interjecting some information about my new granddaughter, Nadia. When I see small children they remind me that Nadia will do those same things when she is their age. Any woman I meet over the age of 50, who looks in any way like a grandmother becomes fair game for me. I am in her face with questions. "Do you have any grandchildren? How old are they? Where do they live?" Of course, I don't really care about the answers to any of these questions. I am just waiting for them to ask me about my grandchild. I am priming the pump.

At a fast food restaurant, I sit in a booth by myself enjoying a hamburger. Activity in the next booth draws my attention. An older couple is dining with a little girl, who is enjoying her hamburger and smearing ketchup all over her face. I try to get the woman to look my way and when she can no longer ignore me, she smiles. This signal is all I need to launch into my story about how I can hardly wait until Nadia is old enough for me to take her out for a hamburger. They ask me how old she is and I admit that she is only one-week-old but I know children grow up too quickly.

I have some shopping to do at the mall, a task that I usually hate, but I find myself in the baby department in a store that I have never before entered. I walk through the racks of tiny hangers and let my hands touch the softness of the gowns and I look at the extravagantly cute dresses that only a grandmother would buy. I have never seen some of these articles of clothing before. What exactly is an "onesie?" And look at this fancy machine that compacts and makes precious little bundles of wet diapers. Times have certainly changed! I do my best to make up for lost time by buying many things.

I am a dangerous woman, fiercely vigilant with a string of pictures as long as my arm. I never tire of telling the same story over and over again. I hear myself and am mystified that one small infant could so easily distract me from everything else I do. I remind myself that this has actually happened to other women before me, but it is hard to take that idea seriously. For this event is so unique, this baby so perfect that I am stunned. This is a cosmic reality to which I alone am privy.

This small baby girl and her calm, beautiful mother, my daughter, have filled huge places in my heart that I didn't know were empty. I want to give them the sun and the moon and the stars but I think that has been done. They already have all those things and more.

I hold this dear one and marvel at her, mouth working as she sleeps. Tiny fingers hold the edge of a blanket. I feast on this small peaceful face. This is an advent for me. For in this small face, I see love, peace, and hope. This birth, all births, hold that promise. Only God could have created the perfect love that we see in the face of an infant. I am reminded of that other birth, so long ago in a stable. I'll bet Mary's mother felt the same way I do. I'll bet she couldn't wait to tell the rest of the family. I'll bet she worried and prayed for her new grandchild. "And he has the cutest way of wrinkling up his nose when he's hungry." "And he has the dearest sweet chin that ..." You have heard all this before? Well, that's what grandmothers do. Welcome to our family, Nadia.

Nurturing God, you set us down in circles of love called families and we live out our days celebrating birth in all the ways we can. Bless our birth and all our rebirths. Amen.

CHRISTMAS PAGEANTS

*And she gave birth to her firstborn son
and wrapped him in bands of cloth, and laid him
in a manger, because there was no place for them
in the inn. Luke 2:7*

I have just returned from the Christmas pageant at church. It doesn't get any better than that. Children and pageants are part of the magic and mystery of this holy season. We never tire of dressing our sweet, rascally children in bathrobes and choir robes to portray the holy family. The love and innocence of our children give us hope even if our human families aren't very holy.

As preacher's kids, our children took their turn in those Christmas programs. And often they were drafted into service when one of the principals came down with the flu. One year, our youngest daughter took on the role of Mary. There wasn't any time to rehearse the role and we trusted Melissa's dramatic sense to do the right thing. The time came for her to lay baby Jesus, a doll from the nursery, into the manger. With no malice intended, Melissa, unceremoniously, slam-dunked baby Jesus into the wooden frame. The congregation snickered as Melissa grinned — a job well done. I was reminded of Melissa and many other Christmas programs, as I wept through the Christmas pageant this morning.

Almost 20 years ago, one Christmas pageant helped to redefine words like "holy" and "family." Nancy had started to attend our small suburban congregation one fall. She had come to stay with folks who lived in the neighborhood. She was young, (she would have been a senior in high school) and in those days she was too pregnant to attend classes. She was also too pregnant to be welcome in her parent's home. She worked at a neighborhood convenience store and waited for the birth of her child.

Our congregation was friendly and usually welcomed strangers and lost souls with open arms, but Nancy's welcome was a tenuous one. Many in the church knew Nancy's parents and were torn between loyalty to their friends and the hospitality they were called to offer. That ugly word "condone" kept edging its way into conversations. If they made her feel at home, would they be condoning her reckless behavior? Would they be jeopardizing the friendships with her parents?

Nancy came regularly to worship and tentatively offered to help in the nursery on several Sundays. The time came for her to be delivered and she gave birth to a baby boy and she named him Joshua, "God saves."

When she returned to worship with baby Joshua, rehearsals were under way for the Christmas pageant. As they were preparing, one of the children remarked that they wouldn't have to use a doll for baby Jesus this year. This year, Joshua could be baby Jesus. What a wonderful idea!

And so it happened on that holy night, that a real baby boy cooed from the make-shift manger. No one dared to speak a condemning word on that night of wonders, but there may have been unspoken thoughts — thoughts of judgment and condemnation. I saw other thoughts there in the manger — thoughts of reconciliation, love, and forgiveness.

Joshua is old enough to have a son of his own by now. I hope that he has grown well and that he has a holy family of his own.

Earthbound God, each Advent, we celebrate
again your coming to us with a human face.
Help us to see you in each human face
that we meet. Amen.

$\mathcal{K}$EITH'S $\mathcal{D}$EATH

*They will hunger no more, and thirst no more;
the sun will not strike them, nor any scorching heat;
for the Lamb at the center of the throne will be their
shepherd, and he will guide them to springs of the
water of life, and God will wipe away every tear
from their eyes. Revelation 7:16-17*

*T*hey buried my friend a couple of weeks ago. He took his life and I wasn't done loving him. There isn't anything else to say, at least anything else to say that makes sense. But then again, death usually doesn't make sense and this death made less sense than most. I am trying to think this out by writing. It won't change anything but words do have power. Maybe they will help.

Keith was a young man, full of talent and winsomeness, with a bright future - a gifted musician with the voice of an angel and fingers born for Widor's "Toccata." When he played the organ, music soared, silence was buoyed up, and the congregation and choir sang better than they could sing.

"What a waste of a life," we say because of course it makes no sense that someone as gifted would not also be perfectly equipped to live a life. Taking one's own life, so final a thing, leaves me breathless, speechless, angry, and sad. We look for reasons — things we could have done — things he could have done — and when all is said and done, all we can say is that he slipped through our fingers. As perverse human beings, when we tell this story we start with how gifted he was. Would the death have been any more acceptable if he had had no gifts? No one to love him? No great future? No talent to share

—

35

with us? Certainly not, but I think we are struck with the contrast here of the brilliant life of music and the irreversible stillness of death.

It wasn't that we didn't see the signs. We all did. And everyone played his or her part well. We recommended counseling. We tried to be the church by surrounding him with our love. We wrote notes — we told him over and over how important he was to us — how his music moved us. We all did our parts but it wasn't enough. We couldn't fill the emptiness in his being; an emptiness that grew and grew until that was all there was of him. The life was gone before death arrived. When all is said and done, he slipped through our fingers.

I want there to be a lesson here but finding a lesson would be too simple a thing. It would tie this sad story up too neatly. This story is all loose ends and raveled edges. But I have a thought or two so we can go on, for now at least. I am reminded to not judge anyone's life by the worst thing they have done. Actually, this is a poor paraphrase of Sister Helen Prejean (*Dead Man Walking*) who fights to abolish capital punishment on the grounds that a person is always worth more than the worst thing they have done.

I am reminded that even though we think we know each other very well, we can never look into another's soul completely. We are strangers to each other in so many ways. In spite of that, we must never stop trying to love our way into others' lives because sometime, we may be able to help an empty soul find its way home.

Whether we can or whether we can't keep someone from slipping through our fingers, I want to try to enjoy every minute we have — every story told, every picture painted, every song sung. It won't change anything about this death but there will be others.

"To the arms of his dear Savior, he shall be conveyed to rest..."
— rest well, Keith.

Merciful God, we stagger among our deaths —
of hopes, of dreams, and the deaths of those
we love. Bring meaning to all our deaths.
Amen.

$\mathcal{S}$HY $\mathcal{H}$ONEST $\mathcal{M}$EN

*For once you were darkness, but now in the Lord
you are light. Live as children of light —
for the fruit of the light is found in all
that is good and right and true. Ephesians 5:8-9*

$\mathcal{S}$hy honest men are hard to find, but at this moment there is
such a man spreading gravel on the road through our woods. Mike
has worked on the road to our cabin for a number of years. It has
been a simple affair — every few years, he comes in after it has
dried up in the spring, grades the ruts, and puts down a new layer of
gravel. The road and Mike have served us well for many years. But
big things are happening in our woods with the anticipation of a new
construction project, so last fall, we spoke to Mike about making a
new straight road that would handle the heavy equipment. We
walked the woods with him, showing him where we wanted the new
road to be. The old twisty, turning road would become a secondary
entrance once the new road was finished. The verbal contract was
struck — he would begin in the spring. He handed us a piece of
tablet paper, showing neat rows of different kinds of gravel. He told
us the price. We agreed.

Early this spring, we were encouraged because one of our neighbors pointed out a large pile of gravel that Mike had delivered to a
spot near our woods. It sat poised for work to begin. But it didn't
begin. About twice a month, we would travel to the cabin and
eagerly turn into the driveway to see if the road was done. It wasn't.
Back home, we would leave messages for Mike on his answering
machine. He never called us back. We worried that he was ill or had
had an accident.

On Tuesday, we arrived at the cabin for our two-week vacation. There was a piece of paper, torn from a tablet, stuck in the door. Written with a heavy lead pencil was this message, "I haven't started the road. I know that you are coming for your two-week vacation. Call me when you get here. Mike"

After we had unpacked, we placed a call, saying that we would be at the cabin all evening. Just as we were sitting down to supper, Mike arrived. He slowly entered the porch with his hat in his hand, his tall, thin body all angles and elbows. He began by apologizing for not getting the work done. Then, he looked us squarely in the eyes and said, "I just couldn't do it the way we had decided. It would cost you too much money. I have an idea — could I show you how I think we should make the road?"

He walked the woods with us, indicating where a couple of trees needed to be cut so that the present road could be straightened. We wouldn't have to build a new road at all. He would be saving us thousands of dollars. We shook on the new plan.

Our culture often doesn't value people like Mike. Most contractors would have gone ahead with the new road and sent us the bill. But because Mike is scrupulously honest and because he runs the business all by himself, he couldn't do a job that wasn't right. It might have been what we thought we wanted, but it wasn't right. And because Mike is a very shy man, it took a lot of effort for him to come to speak to us about the change. He had to work up to it and he had to speak to us in person. He does his job in a way that is good, right, and true.

Today is Thursday and it's raining. Early this morning, we heard Mike's dump truck make his first load of gravel and he has been working steadily ever since. It's time to take him a cup of coffee.

Righteous God, we have trouble doing the right thing, even when we know the right thing. Grant us the courage and patience to do what is good and right and true. Amen.

$\mathcal{T}$WO $\mathcal{D}$AYS $\mathcal{A}$FTER $\mathcal{C}$HRISTMAS

*Then they also will answer, "Lord, when was it that
we saw you hungry or thirsty or a stranger or
naked or sick or in prison, and did not take care of
you?" Then he will answer them, "Truly I tell you,
just as you did not do it to one of the least of these,
you did not do it to me." Matthew 25:44-45*

$\mathcal{T}$'was two days after
    Christmas,
And all through the house
The floor strewn with
    presents —
No room for a mouse.

The children were hyper,
They cry and they whine.
They fight over presents —
"That's mine" and "That's mine."

My husband in PJs
And I in my gown
Were putting our feet up —
Getting unwound.

When out on the porch
Some commotion and noise —
I got up from the couch,
Tripping over new toys.

I went to the door,
Pulling bathrobe real tight,
Peered through the window
Out into the night.

And there on the porch
Stood a family of three —
Three generations,
It looked like to me.

An old grizzled grandpa
Helped a small little tot
And a mother, who looked like
She'd been through a lot.

She leaned on the doorbell,
Then stepped back a pace.
I opened the door
Looked into her face.

"Please ma'am," she said
"Do you have any food?
We've been walking for hours.
We don't mean to be rude."

"How lucky you stopped here."
(With sincerity in it)
"We're Christians —
    we'll help you.
Now just wait a minute."

I closed the door quickly
And said, "Those poor dears.
What's the name of that shelter
Where our church volunteers?

I'll give them directions
So they can be fed.
I'm sure they'll find shelter —
A roof for their head."

The cold air crept in
As I showed them the way.
I felt suddenly tired,
It had been a long day.

I trudged to my bedroom
And reached for the light.
Just two days after Christmas —
That night of all nights.

A night much like this one —
Folks needing a place,
But the rooms were all taken —
Doors slammed in their face.

Just two days after Christmas —
My face burned with shame.
I'd turned away strangers,
My sin was the same

As those who turned away
Jesus and Mary —
No room in my inn.
I'd not let them tarry.

And I'd sent them away
With a greeting so bright
'Happy Christmas to all
and to all a good night.'

*God of the Poor, forgive us when we forget to
see you in the face of the people at our door —
the poor, the sick, the lonely, and the stranger.
Amen.*

$\mathcal{M}$OTHER'S $\mathcal{D}$AY

*Honor your father and your mother, as the LORD
your God commanded you, so that your days may
be long and that it may go well with you in the
land that the LORD your God is giving you.*
Deuteronomy 5:16

*I*n the week before Mother's Day, I spent a lot of time on the
phone and online with four college roommates. The five of us have
remained close friends since our first meeting at Carroll College
in the fall of 1960. If you have done the math, you will see that we
have a lot of years invested in these friendships and each year, these
relationships seem more precious.

This Mother's Day brought us face to face with our inevitable aging
and with the aging of our three mothers and a mother-in-law. All of
them are in health care facilities of one kind or another.

Our conversations went like this:

What are you doing for Mother's Day?

Oh, I am going to leave very early on Sunday morning to pick Mom
up and bring her to the house for the day. We are having dinner and
then I will drive her back around suppertime. We both get worn out,
doing the stairs at our house and even getting in and out of our car
takes a lot of energy. It will be eight hours on the road but Mom
loves getting away for the day.

We have decided to make a special day for each of our mothers, one
on Saturday and the other on Sunday, because we don't think we can
manage them both at the same time. Mom is doing much better since
this last move, but she still confuses easily and the conversation

---

goes better when it's just the three of us talking. The next day we'll spend some time with my mother-in-law. She has just gotten out of the hospital, so we don't know how she will be feeling.

I may try to get Mom out to the house for the day, but it will depend on how her day is going. If she is very agitated, it can be more upsetting to try to bring her to the house. We play it day-by-day.

What are you doing Mother's Day?

One of our mothers is daily challenged by humiliating incontinence, which makes her frightened, withdrawn, and sad.

One of our mothers is suffering with dementia that makes her anxious, frustrated, and mean-spirited at times.

One of our mothers is wheelchair bound and so heartbreakingly cheerful that her loneliness and frustration gets pushed down and unexpressed.

One of our mothers is disoriented, eager, and almost childlike in her acceptance of her situation.

And we daughters are scared, guilty, frustrated, and worn out and worried about our mothers and during the first week in May, because we love and trust each other, we can say to one another, "When do we get to be mothers and not daughters on Mother's Day?" As soon as it is out of our mouths, the other two roommates remind us of the answer — the other two of us who don't have mothers anymore. That's when we get to be mothers on Mother's Day — when we don't have mothers anymore and the thought sticks in our throats and breaks our hearts.

What did we do for Mother's Day? We were able to enjoy our mothers one more day, one more spring day, with flowers blooming and all of us filled with grateful humility for the gift of still being a daughter.

Once again, Happy Mother's Day, Mom!

God of mothers and fathers, our human family
nourishes us and we pray for patience as we
travel through the ages of our life. Bless all
mothers and all who nurture us. Amen.

$\mathcal{C}$OLLEGE $\mathcal{C}$ONNECTIONS

*Now therefore, my son, obey my voice; flee at once
to my brother Laban in Haran, and stay with him
a while, until your brother's fury turns away —
until your brother's anger against you turns away,
and he forgets what you have done to him;
then I will send, and bring you back from there.*
Genesis 27:43-45

$\mathcal{A}$ 40th college reunion is something to celebrate, especially when you can celebrate the event with four friends and their husbands, all still married to each other — all still friends.

Forty-four years ago this fall, I was a freshman at a small college in southeastern Wisconsin. I had been assigned a roommate, Diane, and eagerly looked forward to making new friends and beginning my life as a college student. I wasn't disappointed those first few warm September days in 1960. The friendships came immediately, with four girls at my end of the dorm — Barb, Judy, Kathy, and Sandy. Barb and Sandy each had a roommate as I did, but the five of us hit it off in such a natural, spontaneous way that those first few weeks of what might have been a stress filled time of adjustment, became a fun-filled adventure. Sometime before Thanksgiving, Sandy's room-mate quit college and I moved in with her, getting all the appropriate permissions from housemothers and deans. There wasn't a crisis with Diane and I – we just hadn't developed the kind of relationship that I had developed with Sandy and the others.

This is a long story of an event a very long time ago but the story was on our minds as we gathered for the 40th reunion. As the ten of us were enjoying each other at the reception before dinner, I saw Diane enter the room. I recognized her immediately and left my circle of friends to go and greet her as she entered the banquet hall. She must have recognized me too, because she caught my eye and hurried toward me, her arms extended to me. Taking my hands as she reached me, she said, "I have always wondered why you moved out of my room. I wondered if it was something I had done."

I am not sure that I responded very graciously. I said something about "so many things happening so long ago — so many things forgotten." And we quickly went on to the usual cordial chit-chat of the evening. "Where do you live now?" "How many grandchildren do you have?" "Are you still working?" It was lovely seeing her again.

I would like to have answered in some different way. Perhaps I should have tried to explain what happened. Perhaps I owed her an apology. It stunned me that after 44 years, that would be the first thing she would say to me. I would have liked to ask her some questions. "Had she always wondered why I had moved or did it just occur to her the evening of the reunion?" "Did seeing me bring up some hurt from the past?" "How was she feeling all the rest of our four college years as students?"

Perhaps I should have told her that I always thought she had been relieved when I moved out and she could have the whole room to herself and it had never occurred to me that she might have felt badly about my leaving. But neither of us said any of those things. I enjoyed speaking with her and finding out about her family and her life and I think she enjoyed seeing me again.

As I look back on that evening I am struck once again of how connected we all are. I am awed by how the things we do and say hang in the air between us for 44 years, almost forever. I would like to think that I am better at relationships than I was 44 years ago but my hunch is that there are probably many others that are connected to me in ways that would surprise me and it takes an event like a 40th college reunion to give them voice. I am very grateful for 40th college reunions — it was a great celebration.

God, we are often blind to the effect that we have on others. Give us clarity and tenderness in our relationships with others. Amen.

JASON PRAYING

O LORD, you will hear the desire of the meek;
you will strengthen their heart, you will incline
your ear. Psalm 10:17

I have never written about our youngest son, Jason. Jason is 31 years old and lives independently in an apartment in a small town near where we live. Jason describes himself as being kind of slow and is a man who loves the LA Lakers, astronomy, jigsaw puzzles, and old TV series like "The Dukes of Hazard." He is a faithful man, walking to church every Sunday, bringing his Bible and carefully marking the scripture texts for the day before worship begins. He is friendly, kind, and helpful. He has a good sense of humor.

His life in the church has been rather predictable with parents as pastors but abstract thinking is not his strength. He was confirmed as a teenager but he wouldn't say that he is very good about talking about his faith in God.

Last fall, Jason's grandma had a stroke, from which she has almost fully recovered. Jason had not seen her until she came for the holidays. When she arrived, he ran to the door and wrapped his six-foot frame around his grandma and said, "Oh, grandma, I am so glad that you are OK. I prayed so hard for you." Grandma replied that she thought that was probably why she had come through it so well.

I got to wondering what kind of a God wouldn't listen to a man like Jason? Before I go any further, I must say that I believe that God sometimes answers our prayers in ways that we don't understand and sometimes our prayers for healing don't get answered in ways that we want them to be answered, but I do believe that prayer is a gift that we can offer those we love. Innocent children and folks like Jason may know more about prayer than some of us who pride ourselves on our beautifully worded forms of prayer.

A man like Jason makes me wonder why we think that we have God all figured out when we write our doctrines and our creeds. I wonder why we think that our sophisticated arguments are really eternal matters?

In the 1700's, the founder of the renewed Moravian Church believed that everyone could have a relationship with the Savior. No matter what their status in life was, whether they were married or single or widowed, whether they were infants or old people, or whether they were new to the faith or had been faithful all of their life — all could know the Savior. I also include all of God's children who have special needs, whether they can fully understand faith or whether they are able to express that faith. God comes to all of us in ways that humans can never fully understand.

The capacity to think profoundly is one of God's gifts but thank goodness, there are other gifts that we receive as human beings. The gift of kindness, the gift of caring, the gift of praying for one another can cross language, generational, and intellectual barriers.

All I know for sure is that my world is a better world because of our son, Jason. When I know that he is praying for me, when he calls to just check in, when he cleans off the ice from the stairs so his neighbor won't slip, when he gently helps his other grandma into the car, when he calls to see if we are OK during a storm, I am blessed.

Thank you, Jason.

God of the slow, grant that we might see
beyond our prejudices to the good and true
gifts of all your children. Bless all those who
pray with an open heart. Amen.

$\mathcal{W}$E $\mathcal{K}$NOW $\mathcal{W}$HO $\mathcal{W}$E $\mathcal{A}$RE

*So it was that for an entire year they met with the
church and taught a great many people, and it was
in Antioch that the disciples were first called
"Christians." Acts 11:26*

$\mathcal{S}$everal years ago, my friend and I went on a cruise. The first night
of the cruise we were escorted to our table for dinner. Coming our
way was a young couple who were dressed in Amish plainclothes.
They were seated at our table. Drawing them into conversation, I
asked where they were from. "From a small town in Pennsylvania,"
they said. I replied that my husband had been a pastor for many
years in a small town in Pennsylvania called Lititz. John's face lit up
and said, "that is where we are from." When John and Ann learned
that we were Moravian clergy, they often sought us out as they
enjoyed themselves on this luxurious cruise ship. As we got to know
them better, we learned that they were on their honeymoon and that
their family had given them this cruise as a wedding gift. During the
week, they did it all, enjoying the pool in swimming suits, watching
the shows, and taking part in the day excursions. Only at night for
dinner did they put on their modest plainclothes. The last night, I sat
next to the dear couple. Ann told me quietly that that day would be
the last day that she would ever wear "English" clothes and John
added that he would never shave again, now that he was a married
man. I asked them how it would be for them to go back after this
wonderful week.

"Oh," John said, "our family thinks it's important to experience the
world before we leave it. We call it 'rumspringa' but now we are
ready to make a commitment to our community. You see, we know
who we are."

47

Knowing who we are is a good goal for a life work — knowing who we are as human beings, as men and women, and as Christians. Being settled in our own skin means that we can be more accepting of others.

I think of a young woman in our church who has graduated from high school. She was a good student but people in our small town will remember her because she competed in the national welding tournament, where she took 17th place. She won at the high school and then went on to take first place in the whole state. The fact that she was one of the only girls in the competition didn't seem to faze her. There is a self-confidence in this young woman that is apparent every time she takes the pulpit as a lay leader for worship or as she dons her welding mask.

Knowing what your gifts are and then finding creative ways to use those gifts in constructive ways is an important part of knowing who you are.

Perhaps it is in living the Christian life where knowing who we are is most important. Wearing the name Christian means people will be watching us — to see if we live our lives differently from those who don't wear the name. It should make a difference. It should give us the same kind of confidence that I see exhibited in John and Mary and Jessie — the kind of confidence of knowing who we are.

Knowing God, we search for a way to know who we are — let us rest in the knowledge that we are known by you. It is enough. Amen.

$\mathcal{P}$LACES

Lunch At The Inn

*I therefore, the prisoner in the Lord, beg you to lead
a life worthy of the calling to which you have been
called, with all humility and gentleness, with
patience, bearing with one another in love, making
every effort to maintain the unity of the Spirit in
the bond of peace. Ephesians 4:1-3*

This has been a week of travel and I can usually count on finding something interesting to write about when I am sitting in airports and on airplanes. But my travel had ended and no great story had revealed itself. So after a few hours of mulling over ideas, I went out to lunch. It was a quaint, tourist place, with wait staff in 18th century costumes. I asked for a quiet table, out of the way and pulled out the book I had been reading. The restaurant was a series of very small rooms with long wooden plank tables. Soon after I arrived, three other parties arrived and were seated at tables all around me in the very small room — so much for a quiet place to read.

The couple to my right, a middle-aged man and woman, immediately began their conversation with no attempt to be private. Everyone soon learned that they were old high school friends, getting caught up with each other after a long absence. Two men sat at the table to my left, a young casually dressed man with a nametag from some company around his neck and a man in a business suit. At the third table sat two older men, straight from the golf course or garden, each reaching quickly for the cool glasses of iced tea already on the table.

I tried to concentrate on my book, which was a text about "call," how we understand God's call in our life and what that call can mean for living a meaningful life. It was an interesting book but not nearly as interesting as the conversations going on around me.

The businessman asked, "So what made you go into computers?" The young man launched into a list of reasons: good money, only needed a technical school education, chances for advancement, and then he said, "I just sorta have always liked messing around with computers." I wondered how this young man would react to some of the things I was reading in my book on finding a purpose in your life in an intentional way.

Voices from my right soon drowned out the men's conversation. The man and the woman had been served their food but they ate slowly, pausing between bites to make a point. This was a time for story-telling. The man spoke of coming back to his hometown after the break-up of his marriage. He had stayed in it as long as he could but he finally had to leave. His old friend reached out for his hand and said, "That's OK. You have to realize that we live in a world in which there are people who never do anything they don't want to do." I was just trying to figure out if that was comforting or not when the man responded to her. "I think I am being punished for not answering some kind of call from God." My ears perked up, but the conversation didn't stay with that notion, instead it turned quickly to a political campaign in which they were both involved.

Since I had long ago given up on the reading, I just sat back and enjoyed the last of my coffee and tuned in to the two gentlemen who were obviously enjoying their retirement. One of them said, "I wake up in the morning and there is nothing that I have to do and at the end of the day I haven't done half of it." They both laughed heartily.

Almost reluctantly, I paid for my meal and left before the others. I really did want to hear more but I already felt guilty enough for eavesdropping. Besides, I had all the material that I needed for my sermon on God's call. The sermon, God's word, was somewhere in these good people, struggling to find purpose and meaning in their lives.

It would be a good place to start.

Holy God, we hunger for direction —
for that sense of a life well lived.
Give our lives meaning. Amen.

—

$\mathcal{L}$ET $\mathcal{T}$HE $\mathcal{C}$HILDREN $\mathcal{C}$OME

But Jesus called for them and said, "Let the little
children come to me, and do not stop them; for it is
to such as these that the kingdom of God belongs.
Truly I tell you, whoever does not receive the
kingdom of God as a little child will never enter it."
Luke 18:16-17

*T*he pastor settled himself on the top step at the front of the sanctuary. Children came forward and then settled themselves on either side of him, some lounging on the steps and some sitting straight and tall, facing forward. The pastor acknowledged each one and each child greeted him in return. The children's sermon had begun.

Out of the pastor's pocket came a small collection of magnets, direct from his refrigerator at home. The pastor also brought out a small screwdriver so he could demonstrate how the magnets worked. "See they stick together or to this metal screwdriver," he said.

The children nodded and then in response to his question, began to describe the magnets they had on their own refrigerators. This took quite a long time as each child eagerly shared personal favorites. The pastor fought to get back into the conversation with some information about how magnets work but the children weren't very interested. They quickly went back to telling about their favorite Rug Rats magnet and the magnets that held pictures of them in their soccer outfits.

Finally the pastor again gained control and moved in for the punch line. He asked the big question — "Do you know what would happen if I put this magnet in a drawer for 10 years?" He emphasized the

TEN years. Without missing a beat, one of the little boys immediately said, "it would get lost."

The congregation responded with an uproar of laughter and applause. They hadn't intended to — it was spontaneous.

The pastor tried to gain control again by saying that the magnet wouldn't work any more and that was why people needed to go to church to be near to God and to each other. At least that is what he tried to say but it was difficult to speak over one child's graphic description of the junk drawer in his house where a favorite magnet got all furry and wouldn't work anymore. Other children jumped in with tales of their family junk drawers. The pastor quieted them by asking them to pray and closed the time with a fervent prayer of thanksgiving to God for the children. He walked two of the youngest little ones down the aisle back to their parents. The pastor had survived another children's sermon.

There may have been cynics present in church that morning that wondered why anyone would put himself through such an experience every week. There may have been those who wondered why the pastor bothered or why the parents didn't demand better behavior from their children or why children's sermons had to disrupt the perfectly orderly service of worship. But I know why that pastor bothers.

That pastor does children's sermons every Sunday because he wants the children to know that they belong in their church. He wants them to know that the grownups think they are very important and deserve a special time in the church service just for them. The pastor bothers because he wants the children to experience the soft faces of the congregation as they gaze at their children. The children can see in those faces, the love and the concern and most of all, the hope of the grownups. These are the church's children.

Let the children come.

God of Soft Faces, help us delight in our
children as you delight in each of us.
Let your children come to you. Amen.

$\mathcal{C}$HANGED $\mathcal{M}$Y $\mathcal{N}$AME $\mathcal{T}$O $\mathcal{H}$OPE

*May the God of hope fill you with all joy and peace
in believing, so that you may abound in hope by
the power of the Holy Spirit. Romans 15:13*

$\mathcal{J}$t had been a Bible study like so many other Bible studies, but this time it was on the book of Esther. The theme for the conference had been chosen for me. In my preparation for the study, I was surprised to discover that I had never preached on the book of Esther in all my years of ministry. We read two chapters of this Biblical soap opera each day and the women resonated with Esther as she tried to use her limited power to influence the culture in which she lived. The book ends well and Esther is the heroine who has saved the Jewish people, who could once again live in hope.

After the morning presentation, a woman approached me with her story. She told me that she had a daughter who died at the age of 27. "The months after her death were the hardest I have ever known," she said. "There were days when I could hardly get out of bed. My family and friends helped and most of all, my faith in God helped. One morning, I woke up and the sun was shining and I could actually look forward to the day ahead. It was as if a gift had been given to me and for the first time since her death, I could actually feel hopeful about my life. That very day, I changed my name to 'Hope.' That's what everyone calls me now."

The dictionary says that hope is to want or wish for something with a feeling of confident expectation. This summer I have had the privilege to travel to Europe and South Africa, and I saw hope everywhere. I saw it in the faces of beautiful children living lives that we would see as disadvantaged but they saw as brimming with potential and fun. I saw it in subsistent farmers working their scrubby fields, planting the seeds, and trusting the sun and rain to provide the needed food for their families.

Most of all one image of hope sticks out in my mind. It is a trivial thing but I haven't forgotten it. I was staying in Prague, a beautiful old city, and I was staying in a five-story building that housed a small Moravian congregation in the center of the city. The church was on a street of huge stone buildings, each one connected to the next, all five or six stories, each drawn up to the edge of the sidewalk, just inches away from the narrow street. The buildings were all somber in shades of gray and brown. Some of the buildings were businesses and others were apartments but there were no colorful signs to distinguish them. There was no color at all and even the light from the sky above seemed diffused and weak as I looked out of my window on the fifth floor.

I opened the window and looked out at the scene. There across the street, a few buildings down, I could look into a tiny balcony, where a small window box teetered on the edge of the wrought iron railing. In the window box there were three spindly geraniums and on one of the plants bobbed one bright red flower. It looked like it had absorbed all the available sun on the entire street. In a garden or yard, this tiny bloom would have been overlooked, but here amongst the gray stone buildings, it was a startling image of joy and hope.

Hope is having enough faith and confidence in the future so we can risk living today and finding joy. I think we should all change our name to "Hope."

> *God of Hope, show us the signs of hope that*
> *can stir our hearts. Give us the hope of*
> *abundant life in your son, Jesus. Amen.*

$\mathcal{N}$ADIA'S $\mathcal{B}$IRTHDAY — 9/11

*Lead me to the rock that is higher than I; for you
are my refuge, a strong tower against the enemy.
Let me abide in your tent forever, find refuge under
the shelter of your wings. Psalm 61:2-4*

Today is my granddaughter Nadia's birthday. She will grow up in a
very different world than I imagined for her. It has been a month, a
month yesterday in fact, and I'm still trying to find words to respond
to September 11, 2001. I have been comforted and inspired by the
profound words that others have written, but words aren't coming
easily as I sit down to write today.

Like so many Americans, I haven't lost anyone personally, but I
know someone who has and I think in a very real sense, we have all
lost something very important. We have lost a sense of security and
safety that we have taken for granted for so long.

The most compelling emotion I am feeling is the "mother hen" thing.
I long to have all of my children sitting in my living room and I don't
want them to leave until I say so, until I am sure that it is safe. Fear
has made me plump my feathers and yearn for my loved ones to be
tucked safely under my wings. I have talked with other moms (and
dads) who feel the same way.

Normally, I'm not overprotective. That's the operative word, normally.
It's getting harder to find normal anymore, even though that is what
we are all being encouraged to get back to — get back to normal.
Some days are harder than others.

We have all been inspired by stories of greatness. One friend works at the Red Cross and in the days after 9/11, he was sent to a collection center in downtown Milwaukee. He drives a Red Cross vehicle and told us of stopping at stoplights and having people knocking on the window to hand him money. He also tells this story.

An elderly woman waits patiently in line as people bring forward their contributions. She clutches a small child's hand in each of her hands — a little boy and a little girl. They walk solemnly as the people in front of them hand over a check or a small handful of bills. Finally, it is their turn. She reaches into her purse and takes out a check, giving it to her grandson. He hands it to the Red Cross worker. It is a check for $625. The worker smiles at the little boy and then at the grandmother, who says, "It is their Christmas money." The worker nods. The grandmother continues. "I don't think you understand. It's their Christmas money. It's all the money from their savings accounts, all the money they have received as gifts from our large family since they were born. They wanted to give it to the boys and girls who have lost their mommies and daddies."

I'd like to tell that story to Nadia when she is older. I'd like to tell her the story of the bravery of emergency workers and the kindness of strangers. I'd like to tell her about the goodness of people because I know she'll hear enough stories of 9/11 that will break her heart as they continue to break our hearts.

But today those stories can wait. Today is her first birthday and all she will have to hear today is "Happy Birthday, Nadia, sweet granddaughter."

Loving God, gather us under your wings
and keep us safe in an unsafe world.
Show us your way of peace when we only
know violence and despair. Amen

$\mathcal{Q}$UEEN'S $\mathcal{J}$UBILEE

*For a thousand years in your sight are like
yesterday when it is past, or like a watch in
the night. You sweep them away; they are like a
dream, like grass that is renewed in the morning.*
Psalm 90:4-5

Last week was the jubilee celebration of Queen Elizabeth II's
Coronation. As I watched the golden carriage drive slowly between
long lines of reverent, cheering English folks, I was taken back 50
years to a one-room schoolhouse in rural Wisconsin. I was in the
third grade. Actually I was the third grade all by myself since I was
the only one who happened to be that age in the grade 1-8 school.
I bounced around from reading class to math class and listened in
on whatever was particularly interesting but seldom had a class of
my own.

Our teacher was a miracle worker. Tirelessly, she showed up every
day and managed to teach our motley crew. Tiny first and second-
graders lined up in tiny desks on one side of the room while the older
eighth graders slouched in larger desks by the window. The rest of us
fit somewhere in the middle.

Looking back I can see that Mrs. Rohr was creative as well as
tireless. Because I had lots of time on my hands and because I didn't
sit still very well, she supplied me with names of children with whom
I could be a pen pal. Many of them were in the United States and I
dutifully wrote to them but I was at the schoolhouse early every
morning waiting for those envelopes from exotic cities in Europe.
I don't know where she got the names and addresses but writing
letters and doing research in the worn encyclopedias on the book

shelf in the back of the school room kept me very busy. I was curious about the geography of each country. I wanted to see pictures of the cities that I carefully printed on the plain white envelopes in my third grade cursive writing. The precious stamps were kept in a special envelope, in alphabetical order by country.

I had a favorite pen pal, a ten-year-old girl who lived in London, England. Her name escapes me now but I can conjure up the straight up and down writing on the front of the envelope. We wrote faithfully to each other — of what we did for fun, of our families, of favorite books we had read.

One day, a very special letter arrived. In addition to the usual lined tablet paper was an article torn from a London newspaper. It out-lined the plans for the coronation of the new 26-year-old queen of England. My pen pal wrote of their family plans for watching the parades and almost shyly, she asked me to come to the coronation, if it was OK with my family.

Even after all these years, it amazes me that she would write that. But it was the stuff of our relationship. We shared dreams so it was natural for her to include me in one of her dreams that was soon to come true. The storybook princess who would be crowned a queen had already won the hearts of all little girls.

The invitation arrived at my school in rural Wisconsin. I lived on a farm and had never been out of rural southern Wisconsin. But I had many dreams too and I could imagine myself standing alongside my pen pal friend as the golden carriage passed by. I carefully cut out all of the articles about the coronation in our local paper and tucked them into the envelope with all my stamps in alphabetical order.

Fifty years pass in a blink of an eye. I hope my pen pal friend was standing there on the parade route last week. Happy Jubilee pen pal friend and your Queen Elizabeth.

Lord God, bless the connections we make with strangers, making them friends, across the years and miles of our life. Amen.

$\mathcal{G}$OING $\mathcal{T}$O $\mathcal{C}$AMP

These are the things you must insist on and teach.
Let no one despise your youth, but set the believers
an example in speech and conduct, in love, in
faith, in purity. 1 Timothy 4:11-12

J have just returned from a week of camp, a week with seventy 6th
and 7th graders at our church conference center in Wisconsin. My
body aches and I am counting the hours till I can take a nap. I cannot
imagine what I was thinking when I said "yes" to being the worship
leader for this camp. Apparently I had forgotten what 6th and 7th
graders are like. From this recent experience, I can describe them
as tumbling, frolicking bundles of energy with attention spans of 42
seconds. Their greatest fear is being bored. Here are some other
things that I noticed:

almost anything can be a contest — the cleanest cabin,
the dirtiest cabin, the quietest table.

any contest which involves chocolate pudding or whipped
cream is sure to be a hit.

songs are fun when they are fast and when they are loud.

for girls, the space between the rib cage and the belly button
is now public domain.

I am the age of their grandmothers.

sometimes campers wanted to be four years old and
sometimes, twenty-four.

there are many, many ways to wear a baseball cap.

Those were the obvious things that I noticed — the outside things that make it easy to generalize about young teens. But I learned many other things from these scampy campers. I learned:

behind those mischievous eyes there is much pain, too much pain for such young people.

too many of them are on medications for depression and anxiety.

they are facing issues that most of us didn't face until we were in college.

they are full of wonderful, hard questions that challenged my thinking.

they are intense listeners and enthusiastic participants.

I loved the way they wanted to be in relationship with the staff.

I loved the stories they had to tell.

Mostly, I learned that it is easy to fall in love with 6th and 7th graders and that I am proud that these young people are part of our church. It was in the afternoons when I got to really know them, at the knitting table. Once they had picked up the basics, they settled back in their chairs and enjoyed being in the sacred circle. They talked about their families, about the things they were worried about. They talked about their friends and who was interested in whom. They talked about their faith and their life in the church. I settled back in my chair and enjoyed the conversations, because they were conversations about real matters, about real concerns. It was refreshing, reflective, and deep and I am thinking that the church of the future will be in very good hands if these young people continue to grow as men and women of faith.

Camp next year? I'll have to consider it.

God of the ages, generation after generation,
you lead us. Help us to see in people
of all ages, your gifts and love. Amen.

TIME & SPACE

$\mathcal{Y}$2$\mathcal{K}$ $\mathcal{F}$USS

*Do not fret because of the wicked; do not be envious
of wrongdoers, for they will soon fade like the
grass, and wither like the green herb. Trust in the
LORD, and do good; so you will live in the land,
and enjoy security. Psalm 37:1-3*

$\mathcal{T}$his is my first writing in the year 2000 and I have to say that it
seems to me that this year is very much like the last one, except
for the date thing.

Sitting here safely on this side of 2000, I can smile smugly at all the
fuss that has been made to prepare for the New Year. I contributed
to that fuss. I joined with relish the conversations we had about
whether this is really the beginning of the new millennium or
whether we should wait until 2001. I read with interest about folks
who were stockpiling supplies in their basements. I made copious
notes to make my computer Y2K compliant.

Mostly, I thought the whole business pretty silly. After all, time is a
human construct. So human beings decide how long a year or a
decade or a millennium should be. But then, some of my family members and friends began to report that they had to report to work on
New Year's Eve "just in case." A banker friend reported she had been
to a conference to prepare small banks for the cash flow crisis that
everyone anticipated. Maybe there was something to this hype?

And then the talk would turn theological. There were those who
predicted all kinds of disasters that would take place at the stroke
of midnight, in a cataclysmic judgment. Preachers who had never
preached on "end times" texts felt moved to tackle them.

And if we weren't already scared enough, every week there was a movie that portrayed our doomed planet blowing up, burning up, or getting struck by a meteor.

It wasn't an easy time to preach, but we told ourselves, time is a human construct. What difference does it make to God that one minute before midnight, December 31st, it would be 1999 and the next minute it would be 2000? And we would begin to speak with confidence of God's time and the world's time.

We know the difference. Our generation may care more about time than other generations. We love the new clocks that keep exact time, synchronized with an atomic clock somewhere in the universe. In the past, grandfather clocks probably didn't keep time to the nanosecond but they ticked in a friendly way and chimed the hours. In early Moravian settlements, the church bell rang on each quarter hour, which seemed accurate enough for those hard-working souls.

Psalm 90:4-5 reminds us that God's time and our time are not the same.

With such trust, we marched boldly to the New Year's Eve celebrations. We watched as midnight crept across the planet moving west one hour at a time. And as each midnight occurred, we breathed a sigh of relief and perhaps thanked God for being with us in our anxiety and perhaps asked for forgiveness for our mistrust. As midnight crept closer, we gained confidence and laughed heartily at all the apparently unneeded preparations to survive Y2K. What a fuss!

But having a few extra gallons of bottled water in your basement is not a bad thing, is it? Any day now, I'll get used to the date change and remember to write "2000" in my checkbook.

After all of our preparations, I have found that the only thing in life that wasn't Y2K compliant was me!

Timeless God, we make such a fuss about our human boundaries and limitations. Help us to live and move in our boundless time. Amen.

$\mathcal{T}$WENTY-$\mathcal{F}$OUR $\mathcal{H}$OURS

*Then he said to them, "The sabbath was made
for humankind, and not humankind for the
sabbath; so the Son of Man is lord even of
the sabbath." Mark 2:27-28*

$\mathcal{G}$od gives each of us 24 hours in a day. But an hour isn't always the same length. Some hours drag on forever and others go by much too quickly.

Sunday, 6:00 am — The Sabbath has begun. I read the *Moravian Daily Texts*, go over the sermon for the morning worship, and have breakfast with my hosts for the weekend.

8:45 am — We arrive at the church for the first service of the day. The head usher points to his watch. "I ring the bell at 9:00 am. Better be ready."

10:05 am — The head usher is standing in the aisle, raising his fingers as each minute passes. Five fingers indicate that the service should have been over five minutes ago and I am still preaching.

10:35 am — With coffee cup in hand, I greet folks. Still balancing my Styrofoam cup, I drag my suitcase to the waiting car. We drive to the next church for the second service.

10:55 am — I hang up my coat and grab my Bible and sermon, just in time to walk down the aisle to take my place at the front of the church.

12:15 pm — The pastor and I cut into the head of the line at the potluck dinner. Folks stop by the table to talk. Maybe they remember me from camp? Was I a camp counselor in 1965? They tell me wonderful stories of God working in their lives. I am trying to eat my hot dish. The pastor is waiting at the door to take me to the airport.

1:10 pm — Back on the gravel roads, this time driving well over the speed limit. Or maybe they don't have a speed limit here? Since we can see for 20 miles in any direction, even slowing down for stop signs at the intersections is considered unnecessary.

1:50 pm — I am deposited at the airport where I check in and wait for my 2:30 pm appointment to arrive.

2:30 pm — A young man arrives and begins to tell his story. It is a long story but I am at the airport early and I can be leisurely about the time I give to listen to him.

6:00 pm — It is time to board the plane for Chicago and I settle into my seat. The plane moves away from the gate and then stops. "This is the captain. We have been informed by air traffic controllers that we will have a 90 minute delay, but often it isn't that long, so we will stay out here with the engines running, so that we are ready to go."

7:30 pm — We have been served many beverages and snacks, have talked with one another and both of the pilots. I have finished the book I was reading. I check my watch — there is no way I will make my connection in Chicago.

8:47 pm — I grab my suitcase and begin to run up the jet way and down concourse F. We have landed as far away from concourse B as possible and I have exactly 18 minutes to get to my plane before they close the door. I run and walk and run again. Each departure sign says my flight is "on-time" and I watch in panic as the minutes pass by, this time, much too quickly.

8:49 - 9:01 pm — The smell of Starbuck's coffee wafts past my nose, but there is no time. I pass many restrooms.

9:03 pm — I am getting a catch in my side as I turn the corner to gate 22 where my plane waits.

9:05 pm — The plane isn't on time. In fact, it hasn't even arrived yet. I sit down and try to catch my breath and wait for my heart rate to return to normal. I have plenty of time to do this. The plane leaves at 10:30 pm and I arrive home near midnight.

As I fall into bed, I think — Ah, the restful, renewal of a Sabbath day!

God, how did we get to be so busy? Whew!
It's hard for us to remember your purpose
for our lives in the midst of our busyness.
Grant us Sabbath rest. Amen.

No More Hugs

By the tender mercy of our God, the dawn from on high will break upon us, to give light to those who sit in darkness and in the shadow of death, to guide our feet into the way of peace." Luke 1:78-79

"You won't believe what happened," said my mother as she got into the car for our lunch date. She continued, "they (the staff of the health care facility) took us all down to the dining room for a council meeting. And the director said the most amazing thing. He said that there would be no more hugging. Can you imagine that!? He explained the whole thing and I guess I'll be able to get along but what about those poor people on third floor (the dementia unit)? They will die without hugs."

Trying to be politically correct, I explained to my mom why the director had to do such a thing — that there were probably folks who didn't want to be hugged but couldn't say so — and that this was a way to keep everyone safe. My words sounded hollow and my mom looked at me in disbelief. At almost 92, she just couldn't comprehend the danger. She doesn't know that there are health care facilities where older residents fear their caregivers. She doesn't know about elder abuse. She also doesn't know about the huge lawsuits being charged against such homes. Mom, at 92 doesn't know a lot of fear. Her world is pretty small these days.

Our world is pretty big and most of us, since September 11, 2001, know a whole lot more about fear than we used to. The random acts of violence that we watched happen on that fateful day, make us more fearful. If that could happen, we wonder what other terrible thing could be just around the corner? We hear of the news of the latest things that might just scare us to death. Will it be the West Nile Virus from mosquitoes or Chronic Wasting Disease from eating venison? Will French fries kill us if we don't die from salmonella? Everything seems scarier than it used to.

A year has gone by and we as a nation have tried to respond to the fear — with information, way too much information sometimes, and with security. We hear of the huge, expensive plans to scrutinize every airplane that takes off from one of our airports. By and large, travelers have been cooperative because at least we, as Americans, are doing something. Fear makes us need to protect, lock up, close down. Fear can make us so passive, so withdrawn that we become more vulnerable. Fear can even make us terrorists!

But it would be foolishness not to try to do something. It would be foolish to pretend that 9/11 hasn't happened. It would be foolish to not protect ourselves from mosquito bites or deer meat. (I'm not sure about the French fries.)

That's why the director of my mom's facility needed to tell the staff, "no more hugging." It would be foolish of him to not take care of the institution of which he is in charge.

That's where we live right now — between fear and foolishness. It takes a wise person and a wise nation to know how to balance the risk factors and make choices.

As for my mom, she reports that her "dear ones" — the skilled, kind nurses that care for her — still hug her once in awhile when she really needs it, but she knows that they are very careful about who they hug, so that no one gets hurt. My mom's world has gotten a little bigger and a little scarier than it was. So has our world. May God have mercy on us all.

Wise God, help us walk the shaky line
between fear and foolishness.
Help us to keep safe those we love. Amen.

STOCKHOLM EFFECT

*Blessed are the merciful, for they will receive
mercy. Blessed are the pure in heart, for they will
see God. Blessed are the peacemakers, for they will
be called children of God. Matthew 5:7-9*

I love the way that I can go glibly along, ignoring certain concepts
and issues of my life and then something will happen over and over
again in a very short period of time to make me pay attention. That
happened recently. A "Read and Share" program in our local library
culminated in book discussions all over the city, focusing on the
book, *Bel Canto* by Ann Patchett. *Bel Canto* is loosely based on the
1996 raid on the Japanese Embassy in Lima, Peru, where a large
number of people were kept captive for several months and where
captives and captors began to interact positively with each other,
even playing games of chess. Our conversation about the book had
not gone five minutes before someone mentioned that this story was
an example of the "Stockholm Effect." I had to reach back in my
memory, but it did slowly come back to me.

The term "Stockholm Effect" was coined in the early 70's to describe
the puzzling, completely unpredicted reactions of four bank employ-
ees who became victims of a hostage situation. They were held for
six days by two ex-convicts who continuously threatened their lives
but who also showed them what they later reported as small kindnesses. To the world's surprise, after a relatively short period of time,
all four of the hostages strongly resisted the government's efforts to
rescue them and were quite eager to defend their captors.

Several days later, I read the good news of a young woman from
Utah being returned to her family after many months of being held

captive. The Stockholm Effect was mentioned as explaining the young woman's attitude toward her kidnappers on being returned.

Then we went to war and just days into the fighting, once more, the Stockholm Effect was mentioned in conjunction with some of our soldiers being captured and becoming prisoners of war.

The Stockholm Effect seems to show the human capacity to survive, the complex nature of interactions between captives and captors and the powerful effect violence or the threat of violence can have on human beings. It is easy to romanticize the horror of being kidnapped. We have a need to see even kidnappers or soldiers with some small capacity for doing good, for showing kindness. Many of us can recall the poem about Christmas Eve during one of the World Wars — when both sides stopped the war for a few hours and played a game of soccer together.

The truth is that the kidnapping in Lima, Peru, ended with the violent death of many captives and captors. The young woman's life in Utah has been changed in ways that her family has only begun to understand. And our prisoners of war may be in terrible danger.

I wish that we could stop the war and have a great big soccer game. I wish that enemy could look on enemy with some small capacity for doing good. I wish that nations could shower small kindnesses on each other instead of lobbing huge bombs.

Things like the Stockholm Effect puzzle me but they remind me that we are talking about fragile human beings living in a violent world. It is the human beings that I think about as I watch the news — I hate the destruction and the killing, but I love and pray for all those who continue to work for peace and those who fight in the name of their country.

May God have mercy on us all.

Reconciling God, this world is hard to figure out. We get lost in the complexity. Help us to see your will, not only for us but also for the world. Amen.

𝒯AKING 𝒪FF 𝒴OUR 𝒲ATCH

But I trust in you, O LORD; I say, "You are my
God." My times are in your hand. Psalm 31:14-15

𝑱t is a day off — a day to spend in the woods. I take off my watch and leave it at home on my desk, next to the pile of work needing to be done. All of that work takes time, but not today. Today is my day off.

That little act of taking my watch off is a radical act. It is intentional and it sets me to thinking about time. It sets me to thinking about:

My boss who doesn't wear a watch — how does he do that?

An African saying — Americans have clocks, Africans have time.

A cheery boast on a sundial — "I count only the sunny hours."

A retreat I attended whose theme was "time."

A third grader who has an appointment book with most of the hours filled in.

There is an old cliché that reminds us that we all have the same 24 hours a day to live our lives, but I have discovered that my hours are never the same. Some of them go by so quickly that I know I have been short changed, like the hours of this day off — they will zoom by. An hour spent reading disappears in an instant. I spent five days in an intensive care waiting room, watching the clock. My sister and I could visit my mom for 10 minutes every hour. Those were the longest hours I can remember.

We say to each other that time is a human construct — human beings make the rules about time. In 1582, Pope Gregory set the calendar, at least for the Western part of the world. He ordained that October 4 was to be followed by October 15. Can you imagine this year without those 11 days? The seasonal year was restored to what it had been in 325 and the leap years were readjusted. (For a fascinating discussion of time, see *The Discoverers* by Daniel Boorstin — my husband just happened to be reading this book on our day off and kept reading me sections he loved.)

In case we ever question that human beings make the rules about time, the end of October comes and we turn our clocks back an hour. Just think of that!

I don't have a lot of good advice about time or the use of it. I have, however, noticed two things:

First, I have kept a diary every day of my life since I was 13 years old — just a little four lines for every day. Over and over, I see this pattern in my entries. "Oh, I just dread Tuesday — only four more days — can't wait till Tuesday is over — why did I ever agree to do this?" Then the dreaded Tuesday comes and I either mention what a swell time I had or in some cases don't mention it at all.

Second, I have discovered that it often takes more time for me to worry and fret over the doing of a chore or task than it does to actually do it.

This is the human part of this time business — we live in the hurry and worry of time, in the chronos of time, our time — very seldom do we experience the kairos, God's time. We get glimpses of God's time when we are at peace, when we pause to rest and pray, when we celebrate a sunrise or a sunset, when we garden, when we listen to beautiful music. In a small way we experience kairos when we have a day off, in a golden autumn woods, not wearing a watch. Thanks be to God!

> *Lord God, we get so frazzled trying to keep up,*
> *trying to fit it all in. Help us to find rest in*
> *your time. Amen.*

ΓOOD ΦRIDAY & ΣACRIFICE

*Remember how he told you, while he was still in
Galilee, that "the Son of Man must be handed over
to sinners, and be crucified, and on the third day
rise again." Then they remembered his words, and
returning from the tomb, they told all this to the
eleven and to all the rest. Luke 24:6-9*

Λast Saturday, we took a day trip to our woods to check on the
progress of the building of our retirement home. The plan was that
we would stop at our aunt's house on the way back. We were going
to look at something that needed attention in her yard. We were glad
to be asked to help. In the excitement of the day, we forgot to stop.
We didn't even think about it until the next day. We simply forgot. It
never entered our heads. We felt terrible!

Forgetting important plans, losing our memory, may be one of the
most worrisome things about getting older. My 93-year-old mother
always keeps checking with me — a late night phone call — "I can't
find my Easter cards — didn't I buy some yesterday?" I assured her
that she couldn't find them because she hadn't bought any or at least
I couldn't remember that she had.

We struggle to hold the facts and details of our life in our memory
and we get fearful when those things disappear from our mind,
sometimes not even coming back when we experience a trigger of
sound or smell. It is curious how something we want to remember
can be so easily forgotten and how impossible it is to forget something terrible that keeps going through our minds like a scary movie.

With all these ideas scurrying around in my head, I went to a movie.
"Eternal Sunshine of the Spotless Mind" is a post-modern romp with

an intriguing idea — "what if it were possible to erase a bad experience from our memory?" There are certainly events in my life I would love to have erased from my memory. Perhaps that is why I have so resolutely not attended the movie, "The Passion." I have such a hard time with violent images that I am sure I could not sit through it. But there is this nagging notion as soon as I say that — a notion that that, of course, is the point. Perhaps it is why people are so drawn to this movie. Perhaps it is a good thing for those brutal images to stay in our minds continuously, so none of us can ever forget what Christ has done for us.

Moravians have a tradition of reading the gospel narratives of Christ's passion each day of holy week. Even reading the words is sometimes hard to do, but it would be a poor Easter if I had not lived through the last week of Christ's life by listening once again to the familiar words. In this case, it is good to remember and we purposely remind ourselves with images, with symbols, with hymns, with words, that Christ did indeed die for us. Each time we come to the communion table, we are invited to "do this in remembrance of me." Each time we read the words from the passion narratives, we are invited to "do this in remembrance of me." Perhaps when we see "The Passion" and other films portraying the crucifixion of Jesus, we are invited to do the same thing, to "do this in remembrance of me." I will have to think about that.

May you be blessed in your remembering of what Christ has done for us. It is good to remember — perhaps that is why today is called "Good Friday."

Self-giving God, may we always remember
what you have done for us. We live in the hope
of your sacrifice for us. Amen.

TIME & SPACE

NORTHERN LIGHTS

This will be a sign for you: you will find a child wrapped in bands of cloth and lying in a manger." And suddenly there was with the angel a multitude of the heavenly host, praising God and saying, "Glory to God in the highest heaven, and on earth peace among those whom he favors!" Luke 2:12-14

Several weeks ago, I saw the Northern Lights. Well "saw" isn't exactly the right word. I didn't as much see them as experience them with all my senses. My husband and I had attended a church event and as we stepped into the parking lot for our return home, we saw a small group of folks looking up into the cold winter sky and pointing. They didn't need to point. The sky was filled with light. I knew immediately what the light was, though I had only seen the "Northern Lights" one other time in my life.

Many years ago, while we were at our cabin, I walked out into the summer night and saw some wisps of light. I quickly woke the children and dragged them out to see. To this day, they still don't believe that they were Northern Lights. They are city kids who are sure that it was a beacon from a mall opening or something.

But this was not the kind of light that comes from urban illumination. This was not earthly light. Great bands of light shimmered, with hints of red and blue and green. They moved across the sky but not like clouds that drift, changing shape. These sheets of light pulsed, now here — then suddenly appearing there. They shot through the wispy clouds and lit a lone vapor trail now visible in the night sky. All my senses were on alert. My nose was sure that it could detect a metallic smell. My ears strained to hear some high pitched humming.

Reluctantly, we got into the car to drive the three hours back to our home. I had the luxury of being able to watch them as my husband drove. My eyes were riveted on the magic lights as they flashed outside my window.

Suddenly, my husband slammed on the brakes. The car skidded to a stop. There ahead of us standing in the middle of the road was a huge buck, its antlers silhouetted against the sky. He turned to look at us and then slowly walked off to the side of the road. After that scare, I reluctantly turned my attention to the road ahead so I could help spot other deer that might endanger our small car.

And that's why we both saw it at once — a shooting star directly in front of us, falling straight down towards the dark highway. It disappeared from our eyes just above the horizon.

"And they followed the star to the place where the Christ Child lay." It might have been a night like this. With a choir of angels singing in the Northern Lights and a reindeer looking for his sleigh and a star, a beautiful star, pointing the way home. It was Christmas with all its mystery and majesty. The night made a believer out of me.

God of Mystery, thank you for creating us
with the capacity to experience mystery.
Enrich our journeys with the mystery
of your powerful presence. Amen.

*T*HE *U*NEXPECTED

Now we have received not the spirit of the world,
but the Spirit that is from God, so that we may
understand the gifts bestowed on us by God.
1 Corinthians 2:12

*W*e were going to entertain college friends and wanted to immerse them in the joys of country living so we called the chamber of commerce of our small town. Where could we take them to show off the wonders of "rural life"? Several suggestions were given, and a trip to the local cheese factory was planned but the big event was going to be a cranberry harvest.

The day we went was a glorious fall day, bright blue sky, puffy white clouds, a cool breeze — a perfect day for a cranberry experience. The day was a visual feast with the bright red cranberries floating against the deep green of the bog. We learned how cranberries grow and watched the skilled workers harvest the ruby red fruit. But an unexpected event was even more memorable for me.

As our little van turned off the highway into the lane along the cranberry bog, our driver came to a stop and said "look." There in the lane, not more than ten yards ahead of us, sat a bald eagle. The eagle turned to us and then silently lifted in the air. I had never seen an eagle that close — this was a magnificent bird. After we had recovered a bit, we asked the driver whether he saw the bird often. He teased, "oh, we make him do that every day for the tourists." But then he confessed that he, also, was surprised and delighted at the sight.

Living in the woods has made me aware of the gift of the unexpected. We live with turkey and deer and many beautiful songbirds. But they are totally unpredictable. They don't live by patterns (or more correctly, we humans can't see their patterns) and their sudden appearances thrill the heart.

We humans do strive to have everything in our control — we often live simulated, vicarious lives with the goal that the event is available to us, whenever we want it. Availability is a value — the ability to do things on our schedule and we get irritated when the convenience store closes at midnight and we need to buy milk on the way home from a late movie. We have entertainment available to us 24 hours a day and the ability to record and replay a program when it is convenient for us. I love those conveniences of my life but I love the unexpectedness of the woods too.

As I am getting dressed in the morning, I look out the bedroom window and there is a young deer (yearling) feeding on some tender grass at the corner of the house. I am washing dishes and see the flash of an indigo bunting at the bird feeder. Eating breakfast, we watch a hen turkey taking a dust bath in our sand pile. Even though we see only a fraction of these gifts, if we happen to be looking out the window, they make us feel rich indeed and perhaps they alert us to the rest of our life and other unexpected gifts. God is a God of surprises and perhaps our birds and animals help us to be more open to the other gifts that happen all around us, all the time. As we see kindness and justice and joy expressed in the people we live with I am grateful that I am not in control of everything and pledge to be more mindful of the unexpected gifts and surprises of God.

> *God of surprises, we thrill to the unexpected*
> *surprises of our life. Keep our eyes open to*
> *your hand in all that we see and hear and do.*
> *Amen.*

FOUR-PART HARMONY

As it is, there are many members, yet one body.
The eye cannot say to the hand, "I have no need of
you," nor again the head to the feet, "I have no need
of you." On the contrary, the members of the body
that seem to be weaker are indispensable.
1 Corinthians 12:20-23

I have always loved the story in Acts (Acts 2:1-21) about Pentecost with the flames, the wind, and the confusion of what was happening. Then there is that moment of clarity when all the people speaking different languages can suddenly understand each other.

Several months ago, I attended a worship conference and it was clear at the very first worship experience that this was not a typical Sunday morning congregation. This group of 100 worshippers was made up of many singers, even many tenors and basses. When we sang hymns, the sound was full and beautiful. When left to our own devices on such occasions, Moravians love to sing four-part harmony. We even sing four-part harmony when the rubric in our hymnal advises us to sing in unison, because it is very hard for some folks to sing unison when they love to sing in harmony. We rejoice in the different voices, each singing their own part but coming together in one beautiful voice.

Some of you have heard Garrison Keillor's "Young Lutheran's Guide to the Orchestra." This is an "Old Moravian's Guide to the Choir" or to four-part harmony.

Basses — we begin with the basses because they ground us. Basses sing a lot like tuba players or string basses, simple notes that are the bottom of our beautiful chords. When the bass note is in place, we all feel more secure.

Tenors — tenors can sing very high notes and because tenors would really rather sing the melody, most hymn writers give them very interesting parts to sing, at least that is what altos think.

Altos — altos are like the third clarinet section of the orchestra — you can't really tell what they are singing but it sounds better when they are there. Altos can show you 42 ways to sing middle D.

Sopranos — sopranos have the right of entitlement to the melody and get somewhat irritated when they have to read notes and sing a short section of harmony.

But when these parts all work together, it is such a blessing. The beauty of it is when each individual part can be heard.

I wonder what the church would be like if we listened as carefully to our spoken words — if we were as careful to listen to the different voices spoken as we do the four-part voices? We don't expect altos to sing like sopranos — we don't expect basses to sing tenor parts.

Different voices, different opinions, different ways of speaking make the Body of Christ rich, full, and glorious. When each voice is heard, with respect — with appreciation for what it has to say, then the whole Body is healthy and strong.

Sometimes the Body of Christ sings with one voice — unison — one clear profession and sometimes it sings in four-part harmony.

The kingdom of God is like a congregation singing in harmony with one voice.

God, you give us voices to sing your praises.
Thank you for music and may it be an
instrument of your peace among your people.
Amen.

Missing The Point

*Is not God high in the heavens? See the highest
stars, how lofty they are! Job 22:12*

*L*eading campfire at junior high camp is a risky business. It is a
challenge to speak to seventy-five 6th and 7th graders, seated on
picnic tables, gathered around a smoky fire in the dark. They have
the attention spans of mosquitoes and there are usually plenty of
those, too. Getting their attention and keeping it is difficult. Making
a point that might reach their minds and hearts, nearly impossible.
My little closing talk each evening had been about water, about the
abundance of God's love flowing into our lives like rushing water.

I told a story about a city that had a contaminated well and the
townspeople had to walk a long distance to get fresh water. Quite
unknowingly, one of the young boys went to the old well and put his
bucket way down deep into the well, where the water was still fresh
and good. (Paraphrased from *The Beggar's Bowl* by James
Henderschedt, page 1) The moral of this story is that we should try
to live our lives deeply. I tried to put this abstract idea into something
a little more concrete by suggesting that young people make good
choices by digging deeply. (Even I didn't get this.)

I tried another story. One morning I was walking on our trail, just
enjoying the coolness after an early morning rain. I know that trail
pretty well but I am always on the lookout for a new wild flower or
something that catches my eye and suddenly, there in front of me on
the path was a beautiful rock. It was sparkly and it glistened in the
sun. I don't know much about rocks but I love to look at beautiful
ones, so I picked it up, put it in my jacket pocket and continued on
my walk.

It wasn't until the next day that I remembered my beautiful rock and I went to retrieve it from my pocket. But what a surprise. As I pulled it out, it was just a big old rock — just a plain old brownish, gray rock, indistinguishable from all the other rocks at our place. What had made it beautiful was the wetness from the early morning rain. It was the water that had made it glisten and shine.

I knew I was in trouble when I realized that I didn't have a finish for this evening worship. I was grasping at anything. God can wash away our sins? Water refreshes us?

I looked into the sky for help. All I could see in the dark sky were fast moving clouds — no help there. More muttering — the blessing of water in baptism. How can we keep our baptism vows? I had completely lost them by this time. I looked up into the sky again, and lo! The clouds had moved away and there was a sky filled with stars. Directly over the campfire was the Big Dipper with the cup of the constellation pouring right over the heads of those dear young people. God's blessing poured out upon us. All I needed to do was point and say amen and I did.

Amen.

God of starry skies, you made the stars and the stunning beauty of our world. Help us to live lives that care for your world. Amen.

Suitcase of Treasures

$\mathcal{S}$HOESHINE $\mathcal{K}$IT

*"Or what woman having ten silver coins, if she
loses one of them, does not light a lamp, sweep the
house, and search carefully until she finds it?
When she has found it, she calls together her
friends and neighbors, saying, 'Rejoice with me,
for I have found the coin that I had lost.'"*
Luke 15:8-9

*W*e moved recently, which is to say that we wrapped up everything we owned in white packing paper and stuffed the packages into large cardboard boxes. Being slightly compulsive, we labeled every single box. We labeled them carefully, so that a box that was mostly good dishes was marked "good dishes." We have moved many, many times in our 30 years of ministry, and we pride ourselves on our moving skills.

We arrived at the new parsonage, almost without a hitch. And "hitch" is the operative word. We almost lost the trailer hitch pulling our second car, but that is another story. We arrived with family and friends waiting to help us unpack, which we did in a remarkably short amount of time, with so much help. We looked around our new home with the dishes in the cupboard and the books on the bookshelves and gloated for just a bit at how well we had done.

And then my husband discovered that he couldn't find his shoeshine kit, a kit that he had brought to our marriage so many years ago. It is a sturdy wooden box with a place to put your foot on top and a place inside for all the polishes and cloths you would ever need to keep your shoes shiny. My husband believes in taking care of things and shining the shoes in our family is a task that he has always taken on

—

willingly and with a certain amount of pride. Installation Sunday arrived but the shoeshine kit was nowhere to be found. We made an emergency trip to the grocery store to buy a can of black shoe polish. I assured my husband that this treasure of his would turn up. After all, it was almost as big as a breadbox, all the boxes had been opened, and if he stopped looking for it, it would surely be found. That is my theory about finding things. I also thought to myself he was making a pretty big deal out of misplacing a shoeshine kit!

And then I discovered that my blue bag was missing. Now the moving disorientation had become personal. My sister made me my beautiful bag many years ago. It had a pocket and was just the right size for hauling things. I took it everywhere. It carried my lunch and snacks on a trip. It carried my knitting. It carried a long sleeved shirt and mosquito repellent. I hardly went anywhere without my blue bag. And it was nowhere to be found. I made do with plastic bags from the grocery store but that was very unsatisfying. Mostly, I looked for it, in drawers, on shelves, in stored suitcases, in the basement, in places that I knew it could not be. It was amazing how hugely important that blue bag had become. I began to think how much easier and uncomplicated my life would be if I could just find my blue bag. I dreamed of walking into my bedroom and finding it magically hanging on the doorknob, just waiting to be useful.

I wish I had a happy ending to this story, but I don't. I am writing this having returned from a picnic and having to put away the paper sacks that I had to take my things in. I have become much more sympathetic with my husband and his lost shoeshine kit. I am drawn to the text of the woman looking for the lost coin. I know how she felt. How wonderful it is to know that God is like that woman and that God keeps looking for us in the same way. I guess that's the happy ending.

Seeking God, we so often lose our way and find the strength to keep going because we trust that you are always searching for us. Amen.

—

VALENTINE'S DAY

*Love is patient; love is kind; love is not envious or
boastful or arrogant or rude. It does not insist on
its own way; it is not irritable or resentful; it does
not rejoice in wrongdoing, but rejoices in the truth.
It bears all things, believes all things, hopes all
things, endures all things. Love never ends.*
1 Corinthians 13:4-8

"Buy a three-tier diamond pendant for your Valentine" the TV
commercial pleaded and to further the pitch, we saw a rather
ordinary woman opening a jewelry box in front of an earnest young
man. Immediately, the woman's face beamed with pleasure, her eyes
sparkled and the man looked relieved. The TV voice continued —
"if you love her, show her. Let this lovely gift express your deepest
love." I told my husband I didn't want a three-tier diamond pendant.

This week we have been bombarded by ads for Valentine's Day.
Department stores promise gift selections that express the "Nature
of Love." The discount stores feature costume necklaces that are
"Signs of Affection." Even my favorite grocery store offers "Sweet
Valentine Savings" on standing rib roasts. I told my husband that I
didn't want a standing rib roast, either.

In all the valentine-hype, there is a confidence that the commercial
world has a fix on love — that it's just a matter of buying the right
gift to express love — that this lovely gift can express your deepest
love. I have never found love to be that ostentatious.

In a time of devotions at the seminary recently, a faculty member
spoke of the gestures of faith and it struck me that is how love is

most clearly expressed — in gestures rather than in anything we can buy from a store.

The gestures of love are easy to miss — they are subtle — they are not all experienced in the same way. Some gestures need to be interpreted. Some gestures are very private between lovers.

Here are some of the gestures of love in my life today:

> A picture of my 27-year-old son sitting on the floor, leaning against the couch, with my two-year-old granddaughter's tiny arm around his shoulder.

> My 92-year-old mother calling to see if I got home safely.

> My husband of 39 years smiling at me, as I come through security at the airport after a long day of travel.

> One of our children signing off their voice mail message with a quick "I love you."

> A friend letting me read her new book, before she has even read it.

It does occur to me as I look back to the beginning of this writing, that buying things for the people you love is where you start. Maybe that is an appropriate way to begin a love affair, but as 1 Corinthians 13 reminds us, love grows. The gestures of love come out of a lifetime of loving. They take practice, both in the giving and in the receiving. They come from a lifetime of not only knowing those you love, but also being known by them. Celebrate Valentine's Day by reading 1 Corinthians, Chapter 13 to someone you love.

Happy Valentine's Day.

> *God of love, you show us the power of love.*
> *You love us in spite of ourselves. You love us*
> *before we deserve it. Help us to be lovers as*
> *you love. Amen.*

GIVING A BLESSING

Do not repay evil for evil or abuse for abuse;
but, on the contrary, repay with a blessing. It is for
this that you were called — that you might inherit
a blessing. 1 Peter 3:9-10

Blessings are my business, or at least they are often in my vocabulary as a pastor and as a bishop. I thought I knew quite a bit about blessings since I have been in the church my whole life and have been a pastor for half of my life. I say "God bless you" when someone sneezes and I often use blessing language when I am signing a letter.

But on the first Sunday in June I saw "blessing" in a whole new way. I, along with a colleague at the seminary, had been invited to a congregation in the Midwest to preach. The pastor had invited us to preach a sermon that would raise up church vocations for a very special Graduation Sunday. In this very small congregation, there were nine young persons graduating from high school and the pastor and the boards were honoring the graduates with this special service. From the beginning of the service, it was apparent that these nine young persons were clearly integral parts of the congregation, participating in the choir, ushering, and offering special music.

Midway through the service, the pastor invited all the children to come forward for the children's message. They scrambled up and gathered around the pastor. He also invited all the seniors to come up front and they folded their long legs so they could join the little ones on the chancel steps. Solemnly, he brought out the children's sermon box and invited the children to look inside. A photo was in the bottom of the box but the children weren't sure who the children were in the picture. One child recognized one of the boys and they soon determined that the photo was the graduating class on the day they were confirmed. The children giggled as they pointed out how short some of the boys were then and how tall they were now.

The pastor explained to the children that these nine young men and women would be graduating that afternoon and starting a very new part of their life. He asked them to tell the children about their work and college plans. Everyone agreed that these folks were embarking on new adventures and some of those adventures would be hard and pretty scary. The pastor wondered aloud what the children could give the teenagers to take with them, to help them on their journey. He wondered if they should give them a blessing? The children all nodded their heads very seriously, and so a blessing was given.

The tall young men and beautiful young women took their place, kneeling on the top step of the chancel. All of the little children surrounded them. With great solemnity, they lifted up tiny hands to give a blessing. Many stood on tiptoe as their little hands reached to touch the tall grownup heads. The pastor offered a blessing for these strong, bright church members. But it wasn't his words that offered the blessing – it was the laying on of hands, the way that it is always the laying on of hands. Here the hands were small, but the blessing large.

Surely, God was in that place. Surely, God uses our hands to bless. Surely, God uses the least of us to bless the greatest. Surely, God uses the least of us to bless the rest.

God of Benediction, bless us so that we can become a blessing to others. Shower your blessings on our needy world. Amen.

CANON STAR TYPEWRITER

Are your wonders known in the darkness, or your
saving help in the land of forgetfulness? But I,
O LORD, cry out to you; in the morning my prayer
comes before you. Psalm 88:12-13

Jt had to happen eventually — that day of reckoning, when an email message would pop up innocently: "Your column is due. Are you going to send it soon?" Well, the truth is, I hadn't given a thought to my column, until that message appeared a few minutes ago. I have been on vacation, the wonderful kind of vacation that you return from, groggy and lethargic, rested to the point of unconsciousness. I not only hadn't written a column — I hadn't even remembered that I was supposed to write a column.

I smiled to myself when I thought back to the times I had written columns away from my office, away from all the trappings that make transmission of information so easy and instantaneous. I have faxed them from airports and sent them early by snail mail, just so I wouldn't miss a deadline.

Several years ago, I had noted that a column was due in the middle of my vacation at our cabin in Wisconsin. Those were the days when we illuminated our small log house with kerosene lamps, long before electricity had been brought in from the country road. I did have a laptop computer, which could run on batteries, but no printer or phone line to send the data to the newspaper. I considered going to a friend's in town to write the column, but thought there must be a better way to keep me on my cool, shady, screened-in porch. And there was a better way!

Our oldest daughter graduated from college in 1991 and did what most children do at such a time — she brought to us box after box of her college debris before heading off to Africa with the Peace Corps. Books, clothing, trinkets, and some very heavy clay objects from her pottery course found their way to our attic. Included in the collection was a Canon Star Portable Typewriter, powered by electricity or batteries, leftover from her high school days. At the time, I thought it might be useful at the cabin someday. This was the day.

I opened the box, not sure what I would find — but there it was in all its glory. I rounded up four "C" batteries and turned it on. Amazingly, it still worked. After a couple of decades of computer word processing, it was intriguing to see the little keys strike the paper and actually produce a letter. I began to write my column at the picnic table on the porch. As I kept starting over, I wondered how I had ever finished college or seminary, with papers written on such an antiquated machine. By the time I had completed the column, I had a pile of wadded up paper on the floor. But it was done and now all I needed to do was drive to town to fax it to the newspaper.

I took my work to the local office supply store where a teenager operated the fax machine. He looked at my proud, messy pages, with the crossing out and inked-in added words and I felt compelled to explain that I had typed it on a typewriter. He shrugged and sent the column on its way.

I had asked the editor to fax me back with a response when he received the column. This was his response: "Thanks — but where are you and what piece of equipment did you use to write this column?"

So after all that effort to make sure that my column arrived intact and on time, here I am delivering this two days late. I am grateful for patient and understanding editors. God bless them, everyone.

God of ordinary days, sometimes it is the most
ordinary things that make us smile and give
us a story to tell. Bless our ordinary days.
Amen.

MENDING THE FABRIC OF LIFE

Time to seek, and a time to lose; a time to keep,
and a time to throw away; a time to tear, and a
time to sew. Ecclesiastes 3:6-7

J love to mend. Give me a cold Sunday afternoon on the couch with a pile of mending by my side and I am a happy woman. I love to mend. I have examples of my mending all over the house: a red and white checked tablecloth that wears a large patch covering a spot worn thin by the California sun, a blue jean jacket that is now more patches than jacket hanging in the back hallway. There is such satisfaction in making an article usable again, but mending is getting more difficult.

I used to darn (mend) socks but now the thread used to make socks doesn't respond to darning like the old wool and cotton socks. Hems in my clothing seem to be held together with plastic thread. Maybe my mending days are numbered? I think I am a "repair and make do" kind of woman in a "throw away when it breaks" kind of world. In spite of this, I keep at it even though I admit that mending has its challenges. There is always the moment when I have to decide that all the mending in the world will not fix a favorite shirt. No amount of turning collars (yes, I turn collars — young readers, ask your mother about this) or patching will make the garment wearable. "No one sews a piece of unshrunk cloth on an old cloak for the patch pulls away from the cloak and a worse tear is made." (Matthew 9:16) Even a shrunk piece of cloth can be too much for a piece of fabric that is worn thin. I know this from experience.

I mend anyway, even when I cannot guarantee that the garment will last for any significant amount of time. I mend because it is good practice — it preserves and values old things — it helps me stop the tide of materialism that encourages me to throw away and buy new.

Maybe in some way it helps me to remember that our lives are also fabric. There are many times in our lives when that fabric gets worn and torn. To value our relationships means they may have to be mended sometimes.

When I perform weddings, I try to say to the starry eyed couple: "Remember that your marriage will need to be cared for. It will be very easy to want to discard it at the first sign of age or wear because that is what our culture seems to do, but don't be part of the statistic that half of all marriages will end in divorce. Make mending a part of your practice. Practice mending your blue jean jacket so that you can mend fences, so that you can mend your broken relationships."

Mending is not without its challenges. There is always that moment when I have to decide when all the mending in the world will not fix a favorite shirt or that precious relationship. But until that moment, I will practice mending. I will practice making something usable from something useless, something wearable from something worthless. Maybe my practice will help. There is a pile of mending calling my name.

God of brokenness, our lives get frayed and broken and we need your healing to get our mending done. Mend us, Lord. Amen.

$\mathcal{K}$NITTING

For it was you who formed my inward parts;
you knit me together in my mother's womb.
I praise you, for I am fearfully and
wonderfully made. Psalm 139:13-14

$\mathcal{S}$un streamed into the windows of the retreat center, making slashes of light on metal knitting needles. Yarn made lively circles on the floor, as lengths were pulled for another row. This was a first for me, a daylong knitting retreat. Twenty women had gathered and seventeen of them were knitting as I began. The three who were not knitting sat contentedly among the crafters. Each woman knit her own pattern with her own color and texture of yarn but the knitting felt like a community event.

We began with Bible study, leisurely reading Psalm 139 where God is portrayed as the Great Knitter, knitting us together in our mother's womb. These women knew about knitting and they knew about creation — how a skein of yarn could become something of substance. Making something out of nothing was something they understood.

I had done some reading about knitting and spiritual practice and I shared some of that reading but mostly, we learned from each other. We listened to the stories of knitting and of the knitters and of what they understood to be spiritual about this humble craft. Mothers spoke of knitting large garments for sons and daughters, never knowing for sure that they were appreciated or even worn. Each stitch had been knit with love and a prayer that the scarf or sweater or afghan would wrap the wearer in God's protection.

A mother spoke of arriving in a foreign country to visit her son in the armed forces and finding the knitted afghan spread over his bunk — a talisman of home.

A single woman spoke of the joy of knitting for others. "When my cousin was sick, I didn't know what to do for him, so I knit him an afghan. I think it was a comfort."

Grandmas spoke of knitting tiny sweaters for new babies and of the prayers, hopes, and wishes that were knit into every stitch.

A woman spoke of the very difficult patterned sweater she had knit for her young husband, discovering many years later that he had saved it long after it was wearable.

Several women spoke of knitting 7-inch squares that were sewn together to make lap robes for folks in a nearby nursing home and what a blessing it was to see them in use.

As I look back over the day, here are some of the things that we learned — how knitting helps us in our spiritual practice:

Knitting slows us down. Unless we are working on a very intricate pattern, our bodies relax as we focus on the yarn sliding through our fingers.

Knitting reminds us that we can always start over. Like Jeremiah the potter starting over with clay, stitches can be ripped out and you get another chance to make something precious, like a life.

Knitting reminds us that most times our work can be just good enough. If we make a mistake, we may decide to live with it and praise God that God alone is perfect. In making a sweater and in making a life, most times, good enough is good enough.

Knitting a stitch and saying a prayer and including our love all seem to happen at the same time and the prayers and the love are what really comforts us as we pull our sweater around us or wrap that scarf around our neck. When we surround ourselves with a soft afghan, we are blessed by the knitter and by God, the Great Knitter. Knit one — purl two.

Great Knitter, knit us together as your people
as you have knit us together in our
beginnings. Amen.

$\mathcal{P}$LAYING $\mathcal{T}$HE $\mathcal{C}$LARINET

*Rejoice always, pray without ceasing, give thanks
in all circumstances; for this is the will of God in
Christ Jesus for you. Do not quench the Spirit.
1 Thessalonians 5:16-20*

$\mathcal{I}$ just got home from a junior high band concert. Sitting in the auditorium I was transported back in time. Fifty years ago this spring I was playing in my first 7th grade band concert. The music has improved considerably in 50 years — upbeat rhythms and themes from television and the movies provide good listening. But it was the clarinets that I had my eye on. The clarinets were all girls in the front row to the left of the director and flutes to the right. And oh my, the angst! Coming in, sitting down with perfect band posture, and then the preparation of the reeds. In the mouth, back on the clarinet — is it right? I could never imagine how oboe and bassoon players managed with two reeds. I could barely manage one. I continued to watch the faces of these beautiful young girls. They flinched as their unpredictable instruments got away from them and produced that awful high pitched squawk, but as they had been taught to do, they kept playing, pink and orange flip-flops beating out the time.

I heard other clarinets last night and when the 9th graders played I could see the poise, the confidence, fewer squawks, and the fingers of the girls flew up and down the registers. Such improvement in only two years.

But that's how it works. I started playing the clarinet in the summer before 7th grade so that by fall, I could play a fairly reliable C scale. Three years in junior high, three years in high school, and then two more in college. I can remember myself as a good player. I did play a lot of third clarinet parts but by the time I was in high school I was competing for first chair. I practiced and practiced and I remember being able to play the very complicated clarinet runs in "The 1812 Overture."

Now, my clarinet sits in the bottom shelf of a bookcase in the living room. Several family members have played it over the years. But I can't play it anymore. I tried the other day and I couldn't even get a note out of it. Fifty years is a long time and I have lost many other things too. I no longer can read Greek and I used to be able to. I used to sew clothes for our whole family and now I wouldn't even know how to start. My baritone uke sits in the corner and my fingers can no longer find the chords that used to be second nature to me. Folks reassure me that if I spent a little time, I could pick up these things again. But I don't think it's like riding a bike, which I did try a few weeks ago, after 30 years of not riding. And it's true, I could still do it.

But the things that required practice and hard work do disappear when we stop working on them. Our devotional life is like that. Perhaps that is why it is called a spiritual practice. It takes practice to be able to develop the good habits of Bible reading, prayer, and journal writing. Because what I have learned from playing the clarinet is that no matter how proficient we become, we can lose all the skill and ease we have developed when we stop practicing.

Who knows, maybe I will pick up that old clarinet, or uke, or Greek New Testament, and begin again. Wonder if they would let me in the 7th grade band?

God of achievements, thank you for the
gifts that been given to us and give us
the perseverance to nurture and care for
those gifts. Amen.

STORIES JN THE ORDINARY

Then Jesus said to the Jews who had believed in him, "If you continue in my word, you are truly my disciples; and you will know the truth, and the truth will make you free. John 8:31-32

J was a writer long before I ever published anything. As a third grader, I loved writing to pen pals and my favorite project in fourth grade was making books about the states. We stapled stacks of paper together with a construction paper cover and I wrote pages of information I found out about each state. There were only 48 states then — it didn't take as long. In high school, I wrote for the school newspaper. In college, I was the yearbook editor. I have written in a diary every night of my life since I was 13 years old. And for the last 15 years or so, I have been writing stories.

Someone asked me how I find the stories that I write. The truth is that the stories find me. I collect stories like precious jewels. It's the greatest gift when someone tells me a story. I can't wait to hear them and I love to retell them over and over again. I love the telling part of storytelling but as much fun as the telling is, it is even more fun to write the story down on paper. I love to gather words from the air and from my worn Thesaurus find the exact words to put flesh on the story and let them live on in the reading.

It seems to me that what the world needs now, perhaps more than ever, are good storytellers and good listeners for those stories. This is a very hungry world, not only the overwhelming needs of children who go to bed hungry in this rich country and in the poor world, but also folks who are starving for spiritual food. They are longing for meaning, reaching for something to fill the emptiness. There are many offers of fast food in bookstores filled with endless self-help books. There are books with pseudo-spiritual doctrines guaranteed to bring instant cures for our ills. But they do not satisfy. Our pain is real and the antidotes plentiful. Sometimes what we need is a good story. Good stories do not mask the pain — they tell the truth.

It is not easy to challenge restless, anxious Americans, but I believe that stories can help us think beyond our own small ideologies.

Not happy endings but grace in sad endings.

Not simple answers but confidence in complexity.

Not absolutes but peace in ambiguity.

Not nameless spirituality but deep faith in God, in Jesus Christ.

Because I believe that stories can make a difference, I write them. Even as I do that, I am fearful that I may be contributing to the happy ending/simple answer world-view, that I will contribute to the sappy quotient in the world. I work hard to look for the every day story that challenges and surprises us — stories that aren't predictable, but that can be transformational. I can only hope that writing stories can make things better in some small way. I do believe that stories tell the truth.

God of story, be in our sharing of our
stories and may those stories always point
to your story — the true story of your love
for us in Jesus Christ. Amen.

$\mathcal{T}$WO $\mathcal{S}$MALL $\mathcal{E}$NVELOPES

Whoever is faithful in a very little is faithful
also in much. Luke 16:10

$\mathcal{E}$very six weeks or so, I get two small envelopes in the mail. They arrive within days of each other. Two small, white envelopes with a neatly printed return address label affixed precisely in the left hand corner and a stamp, often the same US 37-cent stamp in the other. The envelopes are from Helen and Ralph. Inside the envelopes are newspaper clippings of my columns that they have carefully cut out of the Friday Express Times newspaper. These envelopes are precious to me. They often contain little notes — "this one made me cry" and "this one reminds me of the time I…"

Ralph and Helen don't know each other — don't live in the same town — but they have both played an important part in my life. Ralph was a member of our congregation several years ago and Helen was a student in a class I taught at Moravian Seminary many years ago.

On separate occasions, they picked up on a comment I made about my mother, although I think the same could be said about most mothers. With all the things that we do in life, often the things that get the most attention are those things that appear in the newspaper. So I mentioned, casually, that my mom liked it when I gave her a clipping of the columns that I had written for the newspaper. Helen began sending me the articles after she graduated from Seminary, many, many years ago. I am embarrassed to say I don't know exactly how many years it has been.

Ralph began sending them when we moved to Wisconsin, five years ago.

I don't know what impresses me more about these two people — their utter faithfulness or their ability to see an opportunity to do a good deed for someone and then acting on it and not doing it once or twice but over and over. It probably doesn't cost much, a 37-cent stamp, an envelope, and an address label but it does take time. It is neither the cost nor the time that is extraordinary, but the consistency of the good deed done for all these years and I hope many more.

This is the kind of thing that I often intend to do but don't quite get done. Most times, I have this great idea to send a clipping to someone, or to send a note to someone or to remember a special gift for someone's birthday, even though we don't usually give birthday gifts but the idea gets lost in the busy. My intentions are good but that is what they usually remain — just intentions.

These two good people, however, took their good intentions and acted on them. I wanted them to know how much I have appreciated their gifts for all these years. This book is dedicated to them.

Hats off to Ralph and Helen!

Faithful God, being faithful is a tall order
for us. We get distracted — we get off course.
Be our guide so that we might be
more faithful. Amen.

SUITCASE OF TREASURES

WRITING IN BOOKS

I have much to write to you, but I would rather not
write with pen and ink; instead I hope to see you
soon, and we will talk together face to face. Peace to
you. The friends send you their greetings. Greet the
friends there, each by name. 3 John 1:13-15

I am reading along eagerly, *The Pearl Diver* by Jeff Talaringo —
light summer fare. It is from the library, carefully encased in clear
plastic, a hard cover book when I am much more accustomed to
reading paperbacks. And then on page 38, they start. Faint pencil
marks begin along the margin, almost invisible, as if the reader felt
badly about having to do it, in a library book. Well, they should feel
badly, shame on them!

But as I continue reading, I begin to be more interested in my secret
mark-maker. While I am reading the story, I am also anticipating the
next pencil mark. Here there is a check mark. I wonder what that
means? There is an underlined phrase in another paragraph. A word
is circled and on another page, the word "42-year-old." I find myself
drawn to these tiny markings and I reread sections trying to imagine
what the reader was thinking. What did the markings point to?

Perhaps he or she is leading a discussion for their reading group and
the marks signify points to make. Or maybe the marks are just to
remind the reader of a particular turn of phrase. Maybe the reader is
a writer or a speech giver or a teacher of literature or a pastor.

I don't want to get moralistic about this but I don't write in books,
library or my own, ever. I can remember the transition from high
school to college, the transition of using someone else's books to

using the ones I had purchased. My freshman year, I actually experimented with writing in my textbooks. I discovered this when I was packing up books from my office and I came across a college religion text and there it was, scandalous, page after page of underlining in bright blue ink. It was dangerous and thrilling. But I stopped doing it almost as soon as I started. The thrill was gone and the harshness of those blue lines of ink convinced me that I was a person who did not write in books.

Which leads me to think about those people who write in their Bibles. I don't write in my Bible, either. I know many, many, faithful, good Christians who joyfully underline, circle, and make notes in the margins of their Bibles, with total abandon. It helps them. It would be impossible for me to do that. Why? Maybe it's a practical matter — I use a NRSV edition with very thin pages and am afraid that the writing would compromise it in some way. But it's probably not a practical matter. It's probably because I am a person who doesn't write in books.

I will confess that once in awhile, when I am reading a novel or an essay, I do get tempted to make a mark, a tiny little check in the upper right hand corner of the page, so I can find the page again. But I don't do it. Perhaps my life would be easier if I did but sometimes you have to take a stand.

And besides, that's why we have post-it notes.

Holy one, we are an eccentric people with strong feelings and preferences. Help us to see in ourselves what it is so easy to see in others. Amen.

FASTING FROM SPENDING

And whenever you fast, do not look dismal, like the
hypocrites, for they disfigure their faces so as to
show others that they are fasting. Truly I tell you,
they have received their reward. But when you fast,
put oil on your head and wash your face, so that
your fasting may be seen not by others but by your
Father who is in secret; and your Father who sees
in secret will reward you. Matthew 6:16-18

We are six weeks into a new year but I am still thinking back to the old one, 2003. Just before 2003 began, last year, I read an intriguing column in the newspaper. It told of the author's attempt to clear out the debris of the previous year and travel more lightly on the earth, without so much stuff. He shared his resolution for the New Year — he would buy nothing in 2003! Well, he would buy groceries and toiletries and gifts for family and friends but he would buy nothing for himself for a whole year. I was fascinated with the idea and decided to give it a try. I thought of it as "fasting from spending" and I am here to report on the experience.

First of all, let me quickly say that this did not come from some higher call from God nor did it even have any kind of self-improvement about it. It just seemed to be something I wanted to try, perhaps as a kind of human experiment. I also must say that I am not by nature a big shopper, so I really didn't expect the experiment would inconvenience me in any substantive way.

It was easy going in the first few weeks of the year, because I had a house full of Christmas presents I was still trying to find space for. And it was winter, so I had all the clothes I needed for the season. As I got to Valentine's Day and St. Patrick's Day I might have gone out and bought a few little decorations but now I really had an excuse not to do that. As spring and warmer weather came, I pulled out my clothes and got very creative about bringing some old duds back to life. I might have looked through the stack of catalogs to see if there was a little something to add to the wardrobe, but now I didn't do that. In fact, some time before summer, I had stopped looking at the catalogs when they arrived in the mail.

Without going through the rest of the year, here are some things I learned:

> Shopping takes a lot of time and I began to feel free about not stopping in a favorite store to see what new things they had for sale.

> If you don't buy anything from a catalog for a year, they stop sending them. No more catalogs meant much more time to read real books and much less poundage of paper to carry off to recycle.

> Speaking of books, one of the biggest expenses in our household is the buying of books. I discovered that the library has all the ones I wanted to read, even though I had to wait for a few weeks to get the best sellers.

> I began to see the things I had in my house in a more meaningful way. I cared for things better. I mended — I repaired — I made do.

To be honest, there were two or three times that I broke my fast. Once when I was stuck at O'Hare Airport and ran out of reading material, I bought a paperback book. Another time, I saw a blanket outside an antique store that matched one I had that was my grandmother's, and I went in and bought it. But the most amazing thing of all is that I didn't need anything, for a whole year. That is embarrassing to admit but it is the truth.

I am not fasting in 2004 — it's probably not good for the economy anyway, but doing it last year was very good for me. And I will probably do it again some day to remind myself that having stuff doesn't guarantee having a life and that with God's providence, what we have is probably enough.

> ***Abundant God, our lives are so full of stuff that we can scarcely breathe. Show us a way to be fed by the abundance of your simplicity. Amen.***

COMING HOME

$\mathcal{T}$HANKSGIVING $\mathcal{B}$LESSINGS

*It is good to give thanks to the LORD, to sing
praises to your name, O Most High; to declare your
steadfast love in the morning, and your
faithfulness by night. Psalm 92:1-2*

"$\mathcal{D}$o you care for more pumpkin pie?"

"No, I have had plenty."

That sums up today, the day after Thanksgiving. Today is the day of leftovers, the day of the overflow of the family feast. For most of us, not all of us, but for most of us, Thanksgiving is a day of plenty. Many of us paused to give thanks to God, even those of us unaccustomed to saying grace on a regular basis. Even the most secular of us can feel religious when surrounded by family and friends, facing a festive table laden with more food than we can possibly eat. It was a day of plenty. As human beings we were moved to say thanks as a response to that plenty.

Thanksgiving is a national holiday and we know what Thanksgiving should look like. We have seen the pictures, year after year — those pictures of clean children, patient parents, and respected elders gathered around the table to eat the fatted turkey. The turkey is golden brown, flanked on either side by mountains of mashed potatoes and gravy, with pies lined up on the side table. The candles flicker and the glasses sparkle.

The pictures that we take of our Thanksgiving won't look quite like that. We will take pictures of families who gather around a table with an empty chair this year. There will be families with fake smiles for the camera, who will be pretending to have a good time. There will be families who have not invited estranged members.

There will be families whose young adults will move the food around on their plates, not able to swallow the dreaded calories. There will be families who will spend the day, quarreling and hurting each other. There will be families who will not have a feast — not even a decent meal of any kind.

On Thanksgiving Day, all of our normal human happenings are heightened. And we try to touch up those pictures to make them as perfect as possible. We try to provide the extra support for the season. There are turkey hot lines to ensure that the bird is moist and tender. Each year, the stores offer more and more Thanksgiving decorations. We gather recipes for the perfect pie.

But with all our preparations, Thanksgiving is in danger of becoming yet another holiday in which we spend too much money, eat and drink too much, and alienate significant numbers of our extended family. We indulge ourselves while our neighbors stand in long lines for their turkey dinner.

So why do we celebrate Thanksgiving year after year? I think it is because in some deep crevice in our heart we need to acknowledge the plenty of our lives. And we grasp at a time to give thanks for the plenty. Yesterday, that plenty seemed spilled out on our tables but in fact it is spilled out in our lives, every day.

God's abundance is so full and rich and we are reservoirs, which are filled and actually overflow. It is fitting that on Thanksgiving we stop and acknowledge that bounteous plenty with our thanks even as we acknowledge that those thanks will always be imperfect.

No matter how hard we try, no matter how much we plan, we will offer to God our imperfect praise and thanksgiving. We will offer our imperfect families, our imperfect intentions, even our imperfect turkeys, and it will be enough.

It will be plenty.

Giving God, thank you for the plenty in
our lives even when we are tempted to feel we
don't have enough. Amen.

*G*OTTA *H*AVE *A* *D*REAM

In the last days it will be, God declares,
that I will pour out my Spirit upon all flesh,
and your sons and your daughters shall prophesy,
and your young men shall see visions,
and your old men shall dream dreams. Acts 2:17

*M*any years ago, my husband and I had a dream. It wasn't a grand dream for world peace, nothing that noble. It was a more modest dream to buy a piece of land with lots of trees on it, build a little cabin and someday live in it.

Over the years, through hard and sad and ordinary times, we worked on the dream. We bought a woods and built a tiny log cabin on it and stole bits of time to travel from wherever we lived to enjoy time there. It was our hiding place. There have been times over the years when the dream was what kept us going. We planned the next summer project in the midst of snowstorms and imagined ourselves sitting on the porch with our feet up when we were overwhelmed with work and illness and stress.

It took the last ten years of drawing plans and making choices to turn a modest log cabin into a modest log home in the woods with all the conveniences that older people depend on. But it happened. We moved into the woods last fall. The "living in it" part of our dream took 30 years. And I have had a few months to think about dreams. This is what I have learned.

It's important to enjoy the process of building a dream all along the way. It isn't only the end result that is life giving.

Dreams can help family stay close as they create common experiences that build closeness.

Dreams can help get you through the hard times.

The capacity to dream is an amazing gift from God. It is a way that God helps human beings make changes that transform the world. With God's help, our young men will see visions and our old men will dream dreams and our young women will see a world at peace and our old women will sit on the porch with their feet up and dream dreams.

The most important thing to know about dreams is that when your dream comes true, you need to have another dream already waiting for fulfillment or many dreams waiting to be lived into. Dreams give us something to lean toward. They keep us looking in the same direction. Dreams give us something to imagine when our minds or spirits need to go on a vacation.

There is a song from "South Pacific" that says it best: "You've got to have a dream — if you don't have a dream, how you gonna have a dream come true?"

So put your feet up, and dream some dreams — your life will be richer and the world will be a better place.

God of vision and dreams, may our dreaming
be acceptable to you and may our dreams
reflect your will for our lives. Amen.

*B*UILDING *A* *H*OUSE

Unless the LORD builds the house, those who build
it labor in vain. Psalm 127:1

I lived in parsonages for 35 years. There was something wonderful about each one of them, something that I loved. We have lived in tiny little bungalows that challenged my creativity to find a place for our very large pine trestle table. We have lived in ranch style houses, one overlooking a beautiful flowing river and another with citrus trees in the back yard. We have lived at the edge of a tiny village where we knew everyone in town. We have lived in a huge mansion of a house on an ancient town square where tourists came knocking on our door on Saturday mornings. The trestle table found its place of honor in each and every one.

I have loved the parsonages but for most of our lives, except for one brief two-year period of owning a house of our own in the 60's, we have put our things in boxes and have placed them in buildings that were not our own. The walls where we tried to hang our pictures were not our walls. Any new holes we made would have to be covered up for the next pastoral family. Sometimes if there were nails still in the walls when we arrived, we tried to match up our pictures and reuse the nails, rather than make new ones. I always cringed when I saw light colored carpeting when we came to visit the parsonage because four children and at least 4 pets were very hard on carpeting, no matter what color it was.

So as we neared retirement and began to plan our retirement home, it was with great joy and excitement. I think I planned a post-parsonage house so that it wouldn't have any of the trouble-some spots that most parsonages have, like sliding doors. Most

parsonages get hard use and sliding doors are often the first thing
to wear out. We usually wore out at least one while we lived in
the house. Sliding shower doors were also vulnerable as were
blinds and shades of any kind. As I planned our new house, it
was intoxicating to pick out kitchen counters that didn't have aqua
boomerangs, put in flooring that didn't have to be vacuumed, and
live in a space that felt like us from top to bottom.

I know that a house is just a building to put your stuff in and it is
people that make a house a home, but being able to live in a space
that smells just right, that has air and lots of light, that has good
bones — oh, what bliss!

My husband has carried a little brass nameplate with "The Aden
Wards" printed on it. He received it from his grandmother years and
years ago and he carried it from parsonage to parsonage all these
years. I knew that we were in our own house when several weeks
after we moved, he took it out to the front porch and with tiny
screws, fastened it by our door. It is a permanent fixture on our
new house. We are permanent fixtures in our new house. No more
traveling for the trestle table. It is in the dining room. What a blessing.

Great Builder, we spend so much time
worrying about how we build our houses.
May we spend as much time on the building
of our faith. Amen.

$\mathcal{T}$HE $\mathcal{H}$EART $\mathcal{I}$S $\mathcal{H}$OME

Do not press me to leave you or to turn back from
following you! Where you go, I will go; where you
lodge, I will lodge; your people shall be my people,
and your God my God. Ruth 1:16

*W*hen it came time to think about a title for this book, one word
just wouldn't go away — the word "home." That is a word with such
warmth and goodness. I couldn't get it out of my head. I have written
about houses but I do know that a home is much more than a house,
much more than a place to put our stuff in. Trying to define what
makes a home is difficult. We might begin by saying that our home
smells right and feels right. It is the place that you go when you are
finished being away. It is the people there or even the people who
used to be there. Home is a feeling, not necessarily a place, certainly
not a building. But the magic of that word — home — is amazing.
After a vacation, when we have seen wondrous things we want to
go home. After a licking, after we have failed, when we have
disappointed everyone including ourselves, we want to go home.

There is no place like home. Home is a place where, when you go
there, they have to take you in. — Robert Frost

I have done a great deal of thinking about the word "home" and
have discovered it means very different things to different people.
For some, it means the house and the people that made up their
childhood. For some, it is geography and the heart quickens when
the car crosses the state line and we read, "Welcome to Ohio." For
some, it is the place not of childhood, but of raising a family, a place
where your own children grew up. For some, it is a mythical place

where things have remained so much the same, that it feels like you never left.

I think for our children, the geography around our woods constitutes home. It is the place we kept coming back to. Whether we were on one coast or the other, we climbed into the car and drove home to the cabin. Now our children are bringing their children and explaining how life used to be here, before plumbing and before electricity. And there is the traveling to touchstones which mean home — the cheese factory, the Easter egg, the railroad tracks, the big oak. Many things have changed but these remain.

For many folks, church becomes a home. When I step into congregations I have known since I was a child, I am home. I remember reading a story about a lost little girl who was rescued by a policeman. He suggested that they drive around and perhaps she would remember where she lived. In a few blocks she spotted her church and told the policeman that she could always find her way home from her church. (*Traveling Mercies*, written by Anne Lamott, page 55)

Finding our way home is all about following our heart where it needs to go. Home is where the heart is. And there can be no more urgent prayer than that all God's children will have a home or a church or a place or a state of mind that means home to them.

Welcome Home.

God, you are home to us. Welcome us into your open arms at our end and grant us the gift of home along our way. Amen.

$\mathcal{W}$RITING 500 $\mathcal{W}$ORDS

We declare to you what was from the beginning, what
we have heard, what we have seen with our eyes,
what we have looked at and touched with our hands,
concerning the word of life — this life was revealed,
and we have seen it and testify to it, and declare to
you the eternal life that was with the Father and was
revealed to us — we declare to you what we have seen
and heard so that you also may have fellowship with
us; and truly our fellowship is with the Father and
with his Son Jesus Christ. We are writing these things
so that our joy may be complete. 1 John 1:1-4

*W*riting has been an important part of my life since I could first
put sentences together on my "Big Chief" tablets that I got at the
dime store, probably for a dime. I write when I am happy and when
I am sad and most feelings in between. Though I love to talk and tell
stories, writing is something that I enjoy in solitude.

Several years ago, I was chatting with a dear bishop who had recently retired. I asked him what he had been doing before coming to the
church meeting. He said that he had been playing the organ most of
the morning. He loved playing the organ and he loved having the time
to do it in retirement. "But you know, there will never be anything as
sweet as the 20 minutes when I used to steal away to play while I
was working."

I know what that dear man meant. One of the joys in retirement is
that I hoped to have more time for writing. But what I fear is that my
writing comes from the people I meet, the places I go, and the experiences that I have. I hope that my compulsion to write won't go away
as I stay closer to home.

Those hours that I used to squeeze out for a few minutes to write were precious.

I used to do my best writing on the run. One night I was stuck at the Atlanta Airport and since I had finished my novel and was too cheap to buy another one at the bookstore, I pulled out my notebook and began to write. I filled page after page and the hours flew by. A short story soon covered the pages.

Another time I needed to prepare a sermon for an ordination service and nothing was coming. I had started several times but it wasn't going anywhere. One night, I found myself on a Greyhound bus, traveling from Chicago because the planes were grounded. I was squashed into a seat by the window with the seat ahead pushed way back. I managed to get to my laptop and with my elbows tucked tightly to my side and the computer on my knees, I wrote happily all the way home.

I have written story plots on napkins and I am an absolute expert at writing sermon outlines on the margins and in between the lines of church bulletins. I hope that people think I am taking notes on the sermon.

It is not only the emotional, passionate things that make writing fun. It's also the physical nature of it. I love to write on paper, always using pencil, never pen. I like the way the lead feels on good paper, smooth, sturdy as the words take hold there.

Writing is a ritual for me in so many ways. Before I go to sleep every night, I write four lines in a diary. It is the practice of thinking about my day that is at first important, but then it is the writing of it — choosing the best words, the most descriptive words, sometimes the shortest words because four lines don't give me much room for going on and on. I save that for my morning writing in a journal where there is all the room I need. Perhaps writing in my diary is good practice for the 500 word essays, which comprise my newspaper columns. I can usually find 500 words to say about almost anything.

Logos, Word God, you are the word for our lives and you provide the words we hear and speak and write. Thank you for being the Good Word come into our world. Amen.

$\mathscr{F}$ORGIVENESS

If we say that we have no sin, we deceive ourselves,
and the truth is not in us. If we confess our sins,
he who is faithful and just will forgive us our sins
and cleanse us from all unrighteousness. If we say
that we have not sinned, we make him a liar, and
his word is not in us. 1 John 1:8-10

$\mathscr{A}$sking forgiveness is not something I think about often. Growing up as a Protestant with good friends who were Roman Catholic, I was fascinated with the idea of confession. My church talked about confession when we were in church but my young friends had to go to a priest and say those words, "Forgive me Father, for I have sinned. It has been 'x' number of days since my last confession." That seemed very dramatic for a young Moravian girl.

One of the earliest gospel stories I learned about forgiveness was the The Prodigal Son or as some call it, The Forgiving Father. That son, that rascal, squandering his money was a favorite Biblical character as we went through confirmation. If that story was right about God and God's forgiveness of our sins, there was hope for me. We learned, "all we like sheep have gone stray" as one of our memory texts.

I was taken back to those early understandings of forgiveness and confession at a recent worship service. The bishop preached on forgiveness. He spoke of the ongoingness of our sins and our constant need for forgiveness. We were challenged to live in a state of confession — of repentance.

"Forgive me, for I have sinned. It's been 1 month since my last confession."

"Forgive me, for I have sinned. It's been 1 week…"

"Forgive me, for I have sinned. It's been 1 day……1 hour….."

Perhaps repentance is an hourly thing or a minute thing. I know that I am constantly speaking and thinking and feeling things that certainly need forgiveness, from God and from other people. My capacity to sin doesn't go away.

Last fall, we bought some pumpkins at the Farmer's Market and they graced our porch steps for many weeks. When they started getting a little soft, I cut them up and left them out for the birds and the turkeys to eat. I scattered them under the birdfeeders and looked forward to watching the big pumpkin seeds getting carried off. Apparently, there is something about this that I don't understand because day after day, the pumpkin seeds lay there, untouched. I saw a couple of turkeys approach them warily. But unsure if they were something to eat or not, they daintily stepped around them. I had every intention of getting rid of that mushy mess but one morning woke to find them frozen to the ground. We looked at them that way for a week or so and then, thankfully, it snowed and the pumpkin mush disappeared, at least until the spring. Once the snow and ice had vanished, they were still there, waiting to be cleaned up. The messes of my life feel like that. Sometimes they get covered up, but ultimately, they are still there. Notice I used the word "messes," which is much easier to write than my sins.

I don't like to use "sin" language. "Gone astray" is acceptable language. It makes it sound like I was really trying to do the right thing but I just drifted off. Sin has so many hard edges to it. It sounds like something other people do, not me. This should be on my refrigerator — "Forgive me God, for I have sinned." I have been sinning. I am going to sin again, probably soon. But oh, the homecoming. Kill the fatted calf for my daughter was lost and now she is found. Hallelujah.

Merciful God, we could not live without your forgiveness. May our confessions to you be often and sincere. Accept our confessions. Amen.

*F*OLDING *C*LOTHES

For God is not unjust; he will not overlook your
work and the love that you showed for his sake in
serving the saints, as you still do. Hebrews 6:10

I have been officially retired for 6 weeks. It feels good. I am very busy and puzzled by the things people say to me when they hear I have retired. Usually they say, "I thought you were retired — you seem busier now than when you were working."

Well, of course I am busy! I am not ill or depressed or otherwise hindered from working, so, of course, I am busy. Busy was never the problem.

When someone feels led to change careers in the middle of their life, we celebrate with them. "Good for you," we say. "You have always wanted to be a writer so congratulations on your hard work to be able to make the change."

That's what retirement feels like to me. It's a career change, in my sixties, instead of in my forties. I have made a career move from seminary administrator to daughter, grandmother, traveler, preacher, and sometime fund-raiser. Of course, I am busy and when I look around at my friends and family who are also retired, they are busy too. I know very few retirees who are sitting on the porch, trying to think of something to do. And I pity the few I can think of who don't have any idea of how to fill their days.

I vowed I would never say "I am so busy — I don't know how I ever found the time to work." That implies a very narrow definition of work as something that you do for which you get paid. This is how the dictionary defines work — work is activity in which one exerts strength or faculties to do or perform something.

Do we think work that is paid for is more important than work that isn't paid for? Is it counted as work if we're enjoying ourselves?

It seems to me that having work to do, whether we get paid for it or not is one of the satisfactions of being alive.

I am very grateful to have work to do in this new phase of my life because I know there might come a time when I won't be able to be busy. It will be one of the losses of aging. (Although my mother at 94 still speaks of being very busy as she participates in all the activities her health care facility has to offer. I hope I can say that at 94!)

Recently I visited an assisted living facility where I was given a tour of the individual rooms for residents, the dining room, activity room, and one small living room with a big long table along one wall. I was curious what the residents did with that long table.

The director said it was for folding clothes. Many of the women moved into the assisted living facility from a life of work, some from farms in the area. When they arrived, they liked visiting the kitchen and the laundry. They asked to help but there are rules that prohibited them from working with the linens for the facility, so they were told they couldn't. But the creative director got permission from some of the residents so these women could help with the folding of their personal items of clothing.

Now these women have work to do. In a small way, their life has purpose again.

They chat congenially and their hands carefully fold the clean clothes as they have done their whole life.

I am retired and I am very busy. Folding clothes is one of my favorite jobs as well.

Holy God, we are grateful for the delicious feeling of falling into bed, tired from a good day of work. Bless all that we do with our minds and our bodies that gives our life purpose and fulfillment. Amen.

$\mathcal{R}$UNNING $\mathcal{O}$UT $\mathcal{O}$F $\mathcal{G}$AS

Again he sets a certain day — "today" — saying
through David much later, in the words already
quoted, "Today, if you hear his voice, do not
harden your hearts." Hebrews 4:7

$\mathcal{J}$t had been a hectic couple of weeks, when work and family collided in one busy event after another. One evening, returning home from a week in California, I unpacked the suitcases, started the laundry, and headed to my office to catch up on email and phone messages. Early the next morning, I jumped back into the car to travel two hours to be with my mother, now 94, who was having some medical procedures at the hospital. It was a long day of worrying about her strength in enduring the test, lifting the wheelchair in and out of the back of the car, waiting for doctors and test results, and finally getting mom back into her room at the health care facility where she lives. We were both tired and a bit cranky. After what she had been through, she had reason to be cranky. I had no excuse.

About 3:00 pm, I said good-bye to mom, stopped for a cold drink with extra ice to keep me awake and called my husband to tell him that I would be home in two hours. I fought drowsiness most of the way but drove without incident. About 20 minutes from home, the car stopped. My new little car with very few miles on it just stopped. The engine quit and I coasted to a little side road where I could safely pull over. It took me several minutes to figure out that I had run out of gas. I was stunned. In 42 years of driving, I had never run out of gas. In fact, I prided myself on taking care of the details. But here I was, 20 minutes from home with an empty tank.

—

I called my husband who said he would come as soon as possible. I assured him that I was safely parked and he should take his time. I did a little deep breathing and tried not to be too hard on myself.

True to his word, my husband arrived, less than a half hour later. He drove up beside my car with his little gas can in hand and said, "You have run out of gas."

"Yes," I said, "that seems obvious."

"No," he said, "I mean you have run out of gas. It's a metaphor. It's time for you to think about retiring."

He was right and so I did. Folks say that God speaks to them in voices and other people. And sometimes God speaks in little human events, like running out of gas.

And so I begin a new exciting stage of my life, with an ache in my heart for the friends who always made my work a joy. But I also look forward to more time with family and friends closer to home and to new challenges in ministry. For now, some of my traveling has come to an end. For now, there will be more time for writing. Thanks be to God.

> *God of our choices, help is to know when to*
> *say "yes" and when to say "no." Help us to*
> *live peacefully in the light of those decisions.*
> *Amen.*

*I*NDEX *T*O *S*CRIPTURES